BEEN THERE, NOTED THAT

Essays In Tribute To Life

BEEN THERE, NOTED THAT

Essays In Tribute To Life

Observations,
Inspiration,
Remembrance,
& Noteworthies
To Share

Stephen Geez

Fresh Ink Group
Guntersville

BEEN THERE, NOTED THAT:
Essays In Tribute To Life
Observations, Inspiration, Remembrance, & Noteworthies To Share

Fresh Ink Group
An Imprint of:
The Fresh Ink Group, LLC
Box 931
Guntersville, AL 35976
Email: info@FreshInkGroup.com
FreshInkGroup.com

Edition 1.0 2012
Edition 2.0 2016
Edition 3.0 2018

Book design by Ann E. Stewart

Cover design by Stephen Geez

Cover art by Moonfire

Cataloging-in-Publication Recommendations
BIO026000   BIOGRAPHY & AUTOBIOGRAPHY / Personal Memoirs
BIO007000   BIOGRAPHY & AUTOBIOGRAPHY / Literary Figures
BIO002000   BIOGRAPHY & AUTOBIOGRAPHY / Cultural, Ethnic & Regional / General

Library of Congress Control Number: 2012932006

Hardcover ISBN-13: 978-1-947867-14-7
Softcover ISBN-13: 978-1-936442-05-8
Ebook ISBN-13: 978-1-936442-86-7

In memory of Mom

I saved this one for you

Acknowledgements

Thanks to the following noteworthy souls:

Team Leader: Ann E. Stewart, Managing Director, The Fresh Ink Group, LLC. *We lost Ann in late 2017. We see her mark in all we do and, especially, how we do it.*

Management Team: Rochelle Sexton

Art/Photo Team: Anik, Joe Posada, D.R. Wagner, Dizzy, Scott Watson, Turtle, Brian J. Smith, Christopher Santino, Moonfire, W.E. Bayn, Geez

Cover Team: Moonfire, Geez

Content Team: Lucas Cale, Beem Weeks, Mark Allen North

Support Team: Kent D. Casey, Todd Tessin, Tom Stockbridge, (the late) Marshall L. Shearer MD, Lendia Buchanan, Dillard Greenwell

Member Team: All of *you* who visit StephenGeez.com, FreshInkGroup.com, GeezWriter.com, and GeezandWeeks.com. It keeps us going when you buy Geez books and spread the good word.

Table of Contents

INTRODUCTORY NOTES

Been There, Noted That features 54 personal-experience essays by novelist Stephen Geez. Written from 1994 to 2010, all are based on true experiences, observations, and opinions. Each features original artwork or photography by contributor-members of Fresh Ink Group, including many fan favorites.

The majority of the essays and the full-color versions of their images have appeared at StephenGeez.com. Some were published elsewhere—often in varying versions—including magazines, newspapers, journals, other websites, and a Chicken Soup book. Many of these essays and their art are have never been posted, appearing in this anthology for the first time. Some of the images used in earlier editions have been replaced with new ones for this 2018 re-issue and the new first-time hardcover edition. All 54 essays have been assembled in response to loyal readers asking for a collection in book form.

Some essay topics may well resonate with you more than others. Some likely will remind you of people who might appreciate your thinking of them as you pass along these sentiments. Three essays convey direct messages you could bookmark and share: appreciation for friendship, birthday wishes, and graduation congratulations. Four offer remembrance, tributes to people Geez has lost, a way to share our search for meaning as we grieve.

If you enjoy this collection, please visit the website and refer your friends and family. Look for the latest material and encores of older classics at the site. Discover Geez novels, heartfelt tales in a variety of genres, all crafted to make us think. Share your thoughts on these essays and other Geez projects via the Contact form through the site. Learn more about Fresh Ink Group's writers, artists, photographers, experts, and more books at FreshInkGroup.com. Authors can find information and support at GeezWriter.com and GeezandWeeks.com.

These narratives range from cautionary tales to poignant pokes at our uniquely human foibles, but all offer chances to celebrate who we are and how much we mean to each other.

Stephen Geez and the Fresh Ink Group appreciate your celebrating with us.

Noted Young

HERE TO FISH

An Essay by
Stephen Geez
StephenGeez.com
Art by D.R. Wagner

"Leave that ol' snake alone!"

Aunt Mary was growing impatient with me, but never before had I seen a snake like that, especially one so big. "Ain't nothin' but a chicken snake. He won't bother you."

I was nine or ten at the time, fascinated by every kind of critter, and known for catching more than a few to bring home. In my neighborhood up north, harmless two-foot garters were my idea of serious snakes, so I'd been sternly warned before embarking on this summer-vacation trip that Tennessee woods seethed with the likes of deadly copperheads, rattlers, cottonmouths, and radiation-hybrid pythonized cobras at least forty feet long . . .

"Leave that snake alone. We're here to fish."

My great-aunt Mary's world impressed me as very different from my own. She and Uncle Carl lived in a ramshackle homestead in the kind of backwoods holler where salamanders sculpt swishes in the mud and hairy spiders bide their time knitting decorative hangings for the outhouse eaves. Mary impressed me as a tough bird—a couple hundred years old, I was pretty sure—who worked hard, honored the Scriptures, and loved her family. To see her eyes sparkle, you need only say, "Would you like to go fish—" Before you could finish the invitation, she'd be piling into the car, ready to roll.

That chicken snake found us along the Tennessee River near New Johnsonville. My father left Mary and me at the end of the old bridge road, a causeway long since abandoned and overgrown, while he and my cousin explored the other side. Mary liked to keep her fishing simple, so as we sat there contentedly amid piles of rocks and great jagged shards of concrete, our state-of-the-art precision gear consisted of cane poles and a bucket.

The sun shimmered low in the sky, dappling the water with swirling sparkles of silver and gold. Weary trees hung over us, weeping the fleeting tears of ephemeral willowflies. Schools of bream and bluegills swarmed in a frenzy below the surface, gorging on the all-you-can-eat willowfly smorgasbord. Catching a pan-sizer simply required reaching up for a fly to thread on the hook, then flipping it onto the water, waiting five seconds, and claiming the prize.

That's when the snake appeared, right out from under my rock.

He was humongous, at least six feet—if not forty feet or more—black as the night, and I'm pretty sure I could see the blood of naïve little boys dripping from his fangs. After Mary's assurance that he engendered no mortal threat, that old snake piqued my interest considerably more than fishing. Using a long stick, I urged him to slither about, then followed him crevice to crack to cubbyhole as his attention gradually shifted from seeking a tasty meal to eluding this nuisance kid.

"Get over here and fish. Leave that ol' snake alone!"

The snake and I paused to eye each other warily. Breaking the tension, I poked him again . . .

And he took off!—a hundred miles an hour straight toward Aunt Mary!

She leapt to her feet, flung the cane pole aside, then snatched up a huge log at least twice her size and proceeded to beat that snake within an inch of his life. The poor feller eventually managed to escape, and we never saw him again. I sat there laughing so hard I couldn't catch my breath.

"You hush now," was all Mary said as she returned to her fishing.

I decided right then that if I were a snake under a rock, I'd want to be warned:

Don't mess with Aunt Mary.

I've always tried to learn from others, searching for meaning in the minutiae of everyday life, those pearls of wisdom that too often slip by unnoticed, so I watched the grown-ups' reactions as I told and retold my Aunt Mary snake story, always earning hearty laughs. Their comments led me to another conclusion:

Advice is easier to give to somebody with a snake under his rock than it is to heed when the snake is under your own.

Many years later I had a chance to go out there with Aunt

Mary again. You can see the causeway from the observation deck at Nathan Bedford State Park, but it's mostly washed away now, eroded by the currents of time and change. There are still places to sit by the water and fish for bream, though, or to reminisce about conquests past. I reminded Mary about that hilarious incident with the chicken snake. She smiled, but I don't think she found it very amusing.

"That snake wasn't botherin' nobody," she said, "until you started pokin' him with that stick." Suddenly, my story had new meaning:

Live and let live.

He'd never have panicked Aunt Mary if I'd not scared him into fleeing.

There's plenty of room in the world for snakes, and they certainly play a vital role in the life cycles along the banks of a river. We were out there catching our dinner and, well, so was he. Too many people spend too much time worrying over how others live, poking each other with all manner of sticks instead of learning how to share a pile of rocks in one little corner of the universe.

The last time I ever saw Aunt Mary was right after Uncle Carl died. My father and I went to see her, and for the first time, this increasingly frail woman didn't light up and wonder if we planned to go fishing. She had some new silk flowers, and she wanted a ride out to Carl's grave.

I'd never visited the old cemetery there in middle-Tennessee, my first chance to see headstones commemorating five generations of kin. Mary pointed out each one, weaving tales about the lifetimes of people I never knew, her eyes glistening with the memories. We picked our way through some tall grass, and I wanted to warn her about snakes, but that story didn't seem so funny anymore, plus I had a lump in my throat, so I let her talk, and I listened.

We cleaned up Carl's grave, clearing the windblown debris that nature scatters indifferently, while Mary stood vigil and nodded approval. I wanted to take her fishing right then, but the time wasn't right. It turned out there would never be another chance.

Mary and Carl are buried side-by-side now, and when I think about that old snake I realize I'd figured out something else listening to her stories and watching her place flowers in honor of the man who'd shared her life. She'd said it that day the snake came around looking for a tasty meal, but I was too young to understand:

"We're here to fish."

I'll bet countless generations of chicken snakes since then have warned their young'ns to watch out for Mary . . .

But it's moments in time that we have to watch for. No matter what you do, or where you go, or how hard you try, there will always be snakes in one form or another crossing your path, and there will be only so many days in a year when sunshine dapples the water while trees weep willowflies and schools of bream gorge . . .

And there will be only so many days in a lifetime when a tough old bird who works hard and loves her family can share this splendor with a grandnephew who lives too far away.

Fish while you can . . .

Then cherish those moments, and don't be distracted by snakes.

SOAKER

An Essay by
Stephen Geez
StephenGeez.com
Art by Dizzy

Yes, the dreaded soaker.

My early elementary years found me living at the edge of

civilization, short tracts of housing plowed through virgin woods, the walk to school punctuated by construction, unfinished roads, myriad excavations, ponds and culverts and all manner of ad hoc standing water, plus our favorite: wide-open ditches. These would freeze and form ersatz skating rinks, lengthy stretches of smooth ice ideal for daredevil sliding, easy and accessible and fun without the danger of drownable depths.

Sure, most kids tended to stay on the path, stick to the walk-way, follow the signs—and here I must specify that this type tended to be, well, the *girls*—but when the greatest risk is but a mere soaker, how can the exuberance of youth dare let so minor a nuisance dampen such thrills?

I recall managing to go for a long time without a soaker. I'd see others earn one in those instants of foot breaking through ice, a leg sliding over the edge, fruitless flailing while water taunts from the nadir of an unplanned slippery slope's slide. Yes, some-body would inevitably step where no child was meant to step—whoosh, swish, slop, shoe waterlogged, sock sopping, pants wick-ing water toward thigh-land, and suddenly that way-cool-if-clunky boot would transform from friend to enemy, its dry twin mocking the loser in all its sanctimonious hauteur of proper use. One of those boots could fill with water instantly, leaving the hapless ad-venturer no easy way to empty it, especially in the suddenly so-much-colder winter freeze.

So the victim of a good snicker-worthy soaker would trudge to high ground and drain as much as possible. If the next stop was school, he would earn a disapproving sigh from the teacher and titters from a few of the dry kids, then have to suffer the awkward discomfort of squish-stepping his way to the very seat under which a puddle would eventually collect, his wrinkly foot wet until time to pull on the betraying boot and head home.

Now, any child in danger of suffering one of these soakers could have carried a small sack with a change of pants and footwear, but nobody at that tender age plans so far ahead. And who really expects to wind up in such an unexpected predicament?

Well, scuba divers do, and skydivers, too. So do hikers and boaters and bikers and climbers and all the adventurers who anticipate needing spare air or extra hoses or reserve chutes or another coil of rope or glue-patches or first-aid kits . . .

And who *doesn't* expect any chance of predicament? Those who have no business getting behind the wheel, people saving money on substandard equipment, reckless souls who think life preservers are too much hassle. Worse, these types are often known for talking friends into joining them for that proverbial slide across the cracked ice, people who ought to know better but too often don't.

See, grown-ups understand that having fun often means something can possibly conceivably worst-case potentially inexplicably go, well, you know, *wrong*. No matter how many times we step into it, no matter how much we depend on the water to fall just below the tops of our boots, that simply won't always be the case. Complacency is no excuse, whether borne of experience, false bravado, or an ingrained pattern of habitual miscalculation. Sometimes it's sheer luck that we manage to avoid a soaker, or even a long series of good-lucks that keep saving us, but sometimes that luck simply runs out.

Some say we should never take a chance, never chase the fun, never even need to wear the boots. Just stay home, they say, the world is a dangerous place. They plop themselves in front of that television plugged into a tangled mass of sparking extension cords, smoke-detector batteries long dead, extinguishers languishing unbought on store shelves, loved ones never having developed a plan for escaping fire.

I say slide down any ditch that's shallow. Carry a change of clothes if the water's just a bit deeper. When it's so deep you might fall through, use the good sense of a smart ice fisherman who monitors conditions, takes ice samples, wears the right outfit, carries the needed gear, and pre-plans all manner of rescue contingencies.

I have another bit of advice, too: Know where the tops of your boots are.

I did get a soaker once, and it caught me completely by surprise. Still, I survived an awkward foot-squishy day, and though I'll never know for sure, I suspect it might have played some small part in keeping me healthy all these years since.

So get out, enjoy life, and indulge your childlike sense of adventure. Yeah, soakers can be a drag, but if they really get you down, buy bigger boots.

Or simply change your perspective. Remember, if that's the worst the world brings your way . . .

Well, sometimes a soaker can be part of the fun.

TOYING AROUND

An Essay by
Stephen Geez
StephenGeez.com
Art by Dizzy

Much as our neighborhood girls liked playing with their dollies, we boys rather found ourselves seriously into cars.

I mean Matchbox Cars. Or Hot Wheels. I could list more brands, but you know the kind I'm talking about: they're still around.

I was more of a Matchbox guy myself, but we didn't discriminate against lads who favored the products of other toymakers. If you brought some cars—or trucks or vans or cool emergency vehicles or even a hearse—you were encouraged to join in.

What we didn't welcome was playing like, well, like girls. Now, I'm no expert about how today's youths toy around—that is, whenever they deign to unplug their virtualities to engage the physical world—but back in the day (read: *way* back) we understood that girls tended to prefer acting out human interactions: faux dating, house-playing, fashion-modeling, career-tasking, or even (ugh!) imaginary tandem spree-shopping. Give any girl a molded-plastic kitchenette, and she could not only spend all day pretending to prepare and serve meals, but she would cajole other girlies into pretending to dine with her.

We boys took a different approach: rather than imagining that some make-believe Lance Lamedork was driving his Matchbox Car to rendezvous with friends for drinks and stimulating repartee about literature and current events, we preferred to direct our attentions toward designing and building the elaborately labyrinthine roadscape that numerous backstory-free, faceless drivers might find themselves navigating.

Think about it. What's the cliché about giving gifts to little boys? They'll likely feign interest as long as their four-minute politeness-spans allow, then set the expensive objects aside and build something out of the box. Watch that same kid for half a century, and I guarantee he'll still be figuratively building his aspirations from ever-bigger potential-unlocking boxes.

I also had a Lionel Train set, one of those Christmas gifts to "grow into," really an excuse for Dad to, you know, help his toddling son "set it up," maybe run it around the track a few times, then run a few more after the kid falls asleep. Though I grew to appreciate that train set, I quickly tired of watching it go round in circles (well, ovals).

Then I discovered its true potential.

I started adding more track. Hey, how about a few crosses?—and a switch or three! Oooo, a tunnel . . . Yes, I rode my bike to many a far-flung garage or yard sale, cheaply mining trainly treasure from those who never quite figured out that playing with locomotives is really about building the biggest, coolest, most-complicated layout that space and materials allow.

Some guys never outgrow that. Eventually they reach the saturation point where bigger is no longer possible, so they focus smaller and smaller until they start finding truth in the details. I mean, some world-shapers look forward to retiring as a chance to indulge just such a "hobby," finally able to afford the time to hand-fashion authentic set pieces: crossing-gates that light and lower, trees that look so real you can smell them, maybe a mountain stream that spills down through a valley crisscrossed by old-style wooden trestles . . .

Now these old boys have the resources to get it just right.

Now they can finish what they started so long ago.

See, our youthful Matchboxing worked best when we could find a huge patch of malleable dirt in which to doze roads, build elevations, erect bridges, craft water features, and even—oh, my heart pounds at the very notion!—maybe even run some switch-back train track through the countryside. We would spend the day relentlessly bending the world to our will, even until dusk frowned upon us, fading light casting long shadows across our land, the proper vehicles positioned appropriately here and there even if they never actually *vroom-vroomed* along the roadways.

Some grownups watch toy commercials to look for gift ideas. Most of us are amused to recognize new versions of our old stalwarts, and we're amazed by "what they can do now." Still, even though society has progressed greatly in blurring gender expectations—an age when boys might aspire to model fashions even as girls grow up to drive NASCAR—we can't help but notice the traditional skew still persisting in our world of toys. The makers and market-targeters know who desires what, and they have a very good idea how and why the wide-eyed young recipients of those realistic little cars like to play.

So the next time you travel by car or train, gaze out the window; or if you board a plane, watch the world pass below. You're witnessing an ever-rearranging gigantic playscape, product of the imaginations of many big little boys, and more than a few ambitious, can-do lady-sized girls, too.

And next time you bark at some kid to put away his toys, look closer at the mess, then appreciate what's really happening.

It might just be a work in progress.

Vroom-vroom!

SNOWBALL'S CHANCE

An Essay by
Stephen Geez
StephenGeez.com
Art by D.R. Wagner

Awakened one morning long ago by the whisper of silence, I rushed to my window and found the world snuggled under a white blanket.

By which I mean snow blanket.

The deepest snowfall I'd ever seen, it beckoned with promises of snowballs to hurl, forts to build, and a towering man eager to fix us with his icy stare.

Yes, I'm talking about a snowman.

Three of us neighborhood boys decided to build one of those carrot-nosed, charcoal-eyed fellers. Ours would be no regular snow-guy, though. No, we planned to build the biggest one you ever saw, a real snow Paul Bunyan, the kind Jack would need a beanstalk to visit. Because small boys are fascinated by big things, and anything worth doing deserves to be done right, we knew our snow Goliath would have to be mega-huge.

We started small, as even the most ambitious projects must, by packing one the size of a softball, then rolling it in circles across the ground, our eyes getting bigger while our snowball grew. Then as our handiwork gained even more weight, we discovered it got harder to push, and we began to realize there's an art to making the perfect ball. It requires constant adjustment, calculating this way and that, twisting and turning to achieve near-perfect round-ness. More than symmetry and esthetics, it became a practical matter. When a snowball begins to outgrow its makers, you have to be extra careful to avoid letting it form any flat spots or it simply won't roll anymore.

Back and forth along the street, over neighbors' lawns, up and down the driveways of grateful shovelers, we appropriated all the loose snow we could find, flouting all geographic and political boundaries, this ephemeral natural resource ours to be exploited.

Our base ready, next came the middle section. We repeated the process for the second level until we had another, not quite as big as the first but otherwise quite perfect—a remarkable achievement, we told ourselves. That's when the laws of physics asserted themselves, those rules of nature that say small boys can't lift huge snowballs, no chance, no way.

Other kids came over to help, neophyte engineers offering ideas more than brawn. We used boards for levers, built a ramp, pressed a red wagon into service, pulled with ropes, and actually had it somewhat off the ground several times, but all to no avail.

That's when one of the wary-eyed local mothers came over

and suggested we abandon our grand plans. Even if we could get our behemoth to stand tall, she warned, it would prove too dangerous. Our friendly snowman might inadvertently topple and crush some unsuspecting playmate.

There were murmurs of conjecture about how the police might arrest a murderous snowman. They'd haul him off for a frustrating and ultimately unsuccessful session of trying to obtain fingerprints, finally discovering the next day that he'd somehow eluded his captors, a mysterious puddle with charcoal and a carrot the only clues to his miraculous escape.

So Plan B kicked in. If we couldn't have the world's biggest snowman, then by gosh we'd make the world's biggest ball.

By which I mean snowball.

So we pushed and pulled, dozens of kids—maybe thousands—all pitching in to help. We added little surprises to the layers, goodies and small toys, the stuff of pockets and junk drawers, building a time capsule that would slowly yield its treasures as our leviathan melted over the coming eons.

It came to rest in my front yard, the biggest snowball ever crafted. Word spread, and people traveled great distances to marvel at our accomplishment. I can't say for sure how big it got because I was still fairly small and most of the world looked rather humongous from my point of view, but I'll guess right now that it grew to at least ten, maybe fifteen storeys high, and unless you have photos to prove otherwise, I'm standing by my claim.

The snowball did last for eons, or at least until long after the blanket of winter had melted away, the freezer season yielding to those first hints of breezy springtime. It shrank, got rather lopsided, lost that former glory, and slowly revealed its long-forgotten hidden surprises. I'd like to think it held fast all summer, maybe until the next winter's snows brought that familiar white playground back to town. Who knows?—maybe, even now, one might still find a small piece of it there in the shade after all these years . . .

But with everything man builds, nature ultimately takes it away. Highways crack and buckle, buildings crumble, bridges fall, and another generation builds its own monuments in their place.

I can't say we learned much from our experience—maybe something about planning and design, thermodynamics and synergy, or pulling together as a team—but we did manage to have quite a ball . . .

Yes, I'm talking about a snowball.

There will always be snow, and there will always be children with grand ideas—even after they've grown up and maybe had a few kids of their own. We were convinced our snowball was something nobody had ever achieved, but records like that are made to be broken—maybe by you or the little ones you love!

So keep that in mind, and the next time you wake up to discover your world is snuggled under a white blanket . . .

Well, you get my drift.

By which I mean snow drift.

SNAKE CHARM

An Essay by
Stephen Geez
StephenGeez.com
Art by Dizzy

Some people are afraid of snakes.

Well, most people are afraid of snakes, or at least wary of

them.

I'm not, and I don't recall any time I ever *was*. As a young lad, I tended to catch them, bring them home, build them warm-light habitats, then enjoy observing them, usually fattening them up and letting them go before cold weather set in. Once I built a wintering burrow to keep a favorite for years, noting how after hibernating he invariably emerged hungry and alert at the first signs of spring.

Mom has never been a fan of snakes. She's never kept them, communed with them, attended their conventions, or supported their causes. She knows snakes play an important role in the eco-system, but she prefers they play it somewhere else.

About the time I was mastering that tricky walking-upright skill, we moved to a burgeoning suburb snaking ribbons of con-crete through virgin forest, an encroachment that ensured our yards would be overrun by confused critters who never saw the eviction notice. Chief among these marauders were toads, frogs, and of course more than a few toad- and frog-eating snakes. In the coming years, I earned quite a reputation and proved myself a neighborhood asset as the lad often called to retrieve and relo-cate an uninvited snakely guest. Too often I would arrive to find a terrified serpent clinging to life inside some form of makeshift sanctuary while the man of the house capered about, armed with all manner of impromptu weapons, his hands and arms already thoroughly fanged. The wisest of these great warriors knew the time had come to step back and let the kid do his job.

So call me The Snake Whisperer.

With snakes, it really is about remaining casual and calm. Peo-ple who whisper to horses and dogs know this. Critters can smell fear, and smell might be the literal term because research suggests that we emit pheromones betraying our innermost thoughts. That's reason enough to avoid playing poker against any beast that gads about on four legs—or on none.

Still, like most people who puff out their chests, snakes really are as afraid of us as we are of them, if not more.

One summer I convinced Mom to let me move my habitat from the garage to the basement, assuring her its serpently tenant would never escape—which he did, promptly, as if he'd always known the way out but had bided time awaiting his chance to get at the snake-hater.

I searched the basement thoroughly while Mom started packing all our belongings and calling real estate agents. I concluded that the snake had taken up residence in a wall under the stairs, the only place where a gap in the paneling would afford easy access. Learning the serpent was "in the walls now!", Mom decided there would be no time to pack, we'd simply have to burn the house and rebuild from scratch.

Eventually I convinced her to come down and beat on the outer wall with a shoe while I waited patiently under the stairs for a scared snake to poke his head out through the hole. My plan required me being out of sight, completely quiet and pheromonally calm, which I found difficult given the temptation to guffaw as she rattled the foundation with such exuberant pounding. I still picture her poised to sprint for safety at even the slightest notion of a snake somehow finding its way out her side of the paneling.

I'd like to describe some epic clash of titans, glory on the battlefield, but the anticlimax here is that eventually the snake stuck his head out, and I ferried him unceremoniously to his home—in the garage.

The following summer the habitat hosted a rescued pine snake. Sometimes called a hog-nose, even known incorrectly as a puff adder, the pine boasts a rather impressive ability to hiss while rising up and flaring its neck cobra-style. Problem was, I couldn't show this off because, like most people who puff out their chests, snakes must feel threatened before putting on such an aggressive display. My snake rather liked me, and he seemed to trust all my pals.

But then he figured out *Mom* was no friend of the snake.

She really didn't like even going out to the garage in those days. As soon as she opened the door that snake would carry on, hissing and flaring, the ersatz cobra sensing that this two-legger would just as soon do away with him and his cushy gig, the all-you-can-eat buffet, daily entertainment, freedom from predators, and rent-free digs.

The pine snake did eventually find a new home in the woods near a river. I hope he enjoyed a long life, well-fed, predator-free, his own warm place in the light. Mom still talks about that old snake that used to hiss at her; even after all these decades he's remembered fondly, which is more than most serpents can say.

If you're deathly afraid of snakes, it might be worth seeking help, such as through systematic desensitization. Usually, the goal is not so much preparing for a career in snake-charming as just learning to be more comfortable around them, or at least in places they're found.

It becomes a small world if you can't go anywhere there might be snakes. It's smaller yet if you have to avoid every place you could find any critter that might bite out of fear.

So if you're in the snake's world and happen across him, just remain calm, then casually move away.

He'll be grateful you did.

And if he's accidentally invaded *your* world, well, I'm sure there's some kid down the street you can call.

CLOWN A ROUND

An Essay by
Stephen Geez
StephenGeez.com
Art by Dizzy

I got to be the clown.

I'm talking about dressing up for Halloween, one of the all-time great holidays.

Way back in the mid-20th century, Halloween in the 'burbs offered a chance for us kids to party, to trick-or-treat, to collect vast quantities of sweets so we might gorge ourselves into pure sugar-mania. It was a time for end-of-summer fairs, haunted houses, spooky hayrides, and nifty decorations in orange and black, all manner of skeletons and ghouls and spiders and bats. It also afforded a way-cool chance to show off, act mysterious, frighten or amuse, or simply play the fool. I'm talking about the costumes, dressing up, masks or face paint, hair and hats, outfits ranging from conservatively tame to outrageously wild.

For me, my favorite was the year I got to be the clown.

Sixth grade, eleven years old, my last chance to participate in the elementary school's autumn festival, I looked forward to the big Halloween event. This was back before such observances grew somewhat restrictive, if not entirely politically incorrect. We transformed the entire public school into a celebratory bazaar, a huge walk-through chamber of horrors, with various rooms devoted to games and entertainment, displays and interactions, and of course the service of food and more food and lots and lots of food. As chairman of the student council, I was charged with greeting arrivals and directing the masses, a roving help-desk to assist and set the tone.

Expected to provide my own costume, I agonized for weeks until Mom found the perfect pattern in a bin at Kmart. After many hours of her painstaking construction, the sewing machine humming, bric-a-brac flying every which way—the kind of mom-mish effort for which I'm still grateful to this day—followed by several shopping trips for accessories and make-up, I became what I considered to be one bodacious cool-ified clown.

Kids had a lot of costumely choices back then, though it seems they have even more now. Many youngsters gravitate toward the currently popular characters, a chance to prove they're in sync with the latest rhythms of pop-culture. Others simply choose their personal favorites, often from a movie or TV show, or maybe (though not so much anymore, Potter notwithstanding) an especially liked book. A few opt for some guise of empowerment, the superhero, wielder of magical powers, conqueror of all fears. Some seize the opportunity to look handsome, or pretty, and to display the myriad trappings comely appearance is perceived to earn. Most want to evoke responses, to unnerve, strike fear, coax irony, or even assert their allegiances through symbols of patriotism, membership, or fandom. For all, though, it's a chance to don the mantle of fantasy, to become something or someone else, if only for a night.

Clowns always struck me as a rather fascinating breed. My earliest memories from TV and trips to the circus are of silly, happy souls. Those who hosted kiddie shows, the ones trying way too hard to be your friend, always proved quick with a laugh, never stingy with the reassuring smiles. But then I noticed that clowns can be sad. What a contradiction, the garish make-up, crazy hair, floppy shoes, and outlandish outfit; but with the smile turned to frown, eyes sorrowful, maybe a teardrop painted where freckles ought to dance.

Surely, then, the clown must have a heart, and when we discover that, the illusion becomes most real. But wait—every child eventually understands that a clown could have simply washed off that make-up, hung up the goofy suit, doffed the fluorescent mane, and stowed the seltzer bottle; so why choose to wear the grease paint even to show he's sad? It's a powerful contradiction, an emotional misdirection, as if to prove that not every second can be happy, so therefore it must be the aggregate of all our feelings that indelibly show who we are. Truth demands to see it all.

I've noticed, too, that it's the sad clown who is least likely to speak, yet somehow finds a way to say the most. It seems most people are quick to share their joys, but reluctant to reveal their pains. That would be an act of trust, one that can't help but speak even without words.

I've known people to display the images of clowns in their homes, often as matched sets, one happy, one sad, a colorfully whimsical update of those thespian masks. I want to say, I hear you. I know exactly what you mean. You can't know one until you've had a chance to meet the other.

The addition of clowns is but one example of how the costumely October holiday has evolved. Rooted in Old World superstitions, myths, and rituals, American Halloween by the mid-20th century had shed its original spiritual pretentions. Unfortunately, some people don't understand that, thinking instead that it's treated even now by casual revelers as some kind of truly supernatural event. They decry the newer secular observances, believing the whole shebang should be shunned—if not outright banned—or at least transformed into strictly interpreted liturgical rites.

I'm happy to report that no one person or group owns our holidays. A bit of research, even a few hours watching The History Channel, reveals how today's popular observances grew largely out of efforts by history's reigning clergy to co-opt longstanding pagan or secular rituals, a way to impose the era's dominant dogma onto deeply rooted traditions. Me, I think it's possible to hunt "Oestre" eggs or enjoy the faces of excited youngsters perched on Santa's lap without diminishing anybody's own personal devotions. I've never known some little boy dressed as Darth Vader, or any young girl outfitted like My Little Mermaid, to consider such fun to be declarations of commitment to serving the dark side.

Still, the holiday I remember from childhood keeps changing with the times. Greater emphasis on safety has led to an increase in organized, supervised events in lieu of knocking on the doors of strangers. Public schools are further removed from the fun, and though I agree that government institutions should avoid any involvement in religious ceremonies, I still think it's possible for a Christmas party to celebrate "Peace on Earth and Goodwill Toward Men" with festive decorations and gift exchanges while leaving any sacred aspects for families and congregations.

Two things about Halloween haven't changed, though: the vigilance required to protect confectionary largess from marauding raiders of the parental or older-sibling sort, and that way-cool part about being the one who gets to choose what he wears, a chance to be anybody or anything one desires.

Costumes come in boxes or off the rack. Many are made by older loved ones, or fashioned by earnest small hands. They're modernized, modified, customized, satirized—even outrageousized. Whether you obtain the one you like or craft your own notions into a fully realized visual statement, you put it on and discover how it ignites the imagination. That, my friends, is one of the great things about life.

Dressing up reminds us we should never forget to seek out opportunities for fun, even when—especially when—times are bad. Many things about my world have proven painful, and harsh tragedies have touched the spheres of those I care for most. Too often our faces can't help but reveal the sadness. But every heartache seems balanced by triumph, those rare, serendipitous moments of joy. It's a beautiful world, and even loss means surely we must have loved, which leaves memories that eventually ought to chase away the frowns.

I look at the sad clown, and I think he knows all this, and he's saying it's okay to feel the hurts, to show others how hard it can sometimes be.

And I watch the happy clown and wonder, Doesn't he know that living even the best life can—and sometimes will—prove near-overwhelmingly hard? Maybe he *does* know, and he's decided to walk ahead, to face the worst, then look back toward us and offer his most reassuring smile.

Then blast us one more time with that seltzer bottle, just to keep it real.

Yes, some clowns can touch your soul. Others will make you laugh. I think the best ones find a way to do both.

So what will you be for Halloween?

Me, I like to be the clown.

SOMETHING I NEED

An Essay by
Stephen Geez
StephenGeez.com
Image by Geez

It was something I just needed to have.

Barely twelve at the time, I had just embarked on the whole

junior-high experience in an era of long-long hair and hippie regalia: bell bottoms, wide belts with oversized buckles, message t-shirts, fringed vests, medallions, floppy hats, head bands, sandals and earth shoes, rock-band patches, roach-clip necklaces, beaded bracelets (guys, too), and gaudy finger rings featuring new-age symbols. (Okay, mood rings colored our world briefly, too—until we came to our senses.)

On a weekend when Uncle Bob and Aunt Doris drove up to stay with us a few days, I rode my bike to Kmart to look for rings akin to the styles several of the cooler guys had been sporting at school. I did find a nice selection, metallic designs fastened to variously shaped wood backings, but they proved a bit costly for someone my age, even with my short list of obligations not yet including mortgage payments, groceries, and car insurance. I saw no point in shopping around since Kmart would have as good a deal as anyone, this being an era of competition by price, quality, and brands as opposed to predatory loss-leading, exclusive contracting, and importing from some communist powerhouse building its economy largely on theft of technology and intellectual property rights.

So I gave up on the notion of sporting my own fingerware until I saw my friend Dave hanging out at the playground near his house. He showed me a boxful of the same kind of rings, several different styles, priced to move well below retail. Seems he had a secret wholesale source he declined to reveal. Well, did I want one or not?

Of course, I did.

Intent on joining the ranks of the cool-fingered, pleased with providence for the opportunity to afford some stylin' gear, I went home to gather my funds. Remember, a ring was something I just needed to have.

Uncle Bob noticed I'd undertaken a mission, and that piqued his curiosity.

One of Bob's many characteristics I still recall fondly more than twenty-five years since losing him is that he paid attention. He always showed interest, asked questions, offered opinions, and respected whatever outlandish nonsense I felt compelled to say. He quickly grew so fascinated by the notion of symbol rings for guys that he urged me into his Caddie for a trip to Kmart to see them for himself.

He did seem impressed by the rings, though now it seems the only thing he could like about such silly contrivances would be my interest in them.

He made me an offer on the spot: Pick any one I liked, and he would buy it for me, my only obligation being to wash his Caddie later that day. Yes, I could wear my ring home.

I would have come out way ahead on that deal, the ring costing more than a car wash would be worth, especially since his car didn't even need a wash. I passed, though—graciously, gratefully. I couldn't see him spending so much of his hard-earned cash doing me a favor when I had an easier deal and a better way to get a ring on my own.

However, Bob had figured out something I was still missing, and he didn't want to let it go.

He wondered if Dave's selection included every design. Well, no, but he did have two I liked. Bob wondered if Kmart's selection included any I liked even better than Dave's. Well . . . sure. Dave didn't have the one with the wood backing cut into the shape of a star. Still, for the price, Dave did offer some I liked plenty.

Satisfied, Bob herded me toward the exit. Then during the drive home, he made me another offer: If I would refuse to settle for any less than the star-backed ring, he would wait until I checked to see if Dave could get it for me. If Dave couldn't, Bob would buy it himself from Kmart and sell it to me for Dave's price, no car-wash required. Well, okay, sure. After all, it *was* something I just needed to have.

Dave came by my house that afternoon with the box of rings. Disappointed I'd settled on a different design, he pitched me for several minutes, even offering to lower the price on my alternate choice. Finally, he relented and agreed to bring me the star one in a day or two.

And that's when I figured out his supply chain.

Okay, it didn't dawn on me as fast as Bob might have hoped, but it's a sure bet he knew I would figure it out eventually.

Now, much as I'd like to say my first impulse was to do the right thing, I can't. I fooled myself into thinking Dave somehow deserved the business. Look at all the effort he'd put into the sale, even offering in-home shopping and custom procurement.

Well, Bob didn't see it that way. Not even close.

I argued that I wasn't the one shoplifting, and that Dave was doing it with or without my purchase anyway.

The whole doing-it-anyway notion didn't fly at all. Dave didn't have a boxful of rings because he wanted them for himself. He acquired those rings with the intention of selling them for cash, an illicit business model that works only if people are willing to buy. Bob didn't see much difference between stealing and having someone else steal for me. Finally it made sense to me that there really is no difference between doing wrong and being the reason someone else does wrong.

Actually, Bob pointed out, the latter is even worse. You buy stolen goods, you're a thief. You buy them from a friend, you're a thief and a bad friend.

Seriously: What kind of person looks the other way when a friend is messing up? What kind of person *encourages* a friend to shoplift? What kind of person pays a friend to steal?

Okay, it took me twelve-odd years to come to that realization. Even so, I find it galling to think how many adults never figure it out. Just this morning I listened to a guy explaining why it's okay to purchase bootlegs of pirated movies from his friend, then sell them over the internet. I'd like to see him run that one by Uncle Bob.

Too many decades have passed since the ring episode, but I do like to think I've spent those years encouraging my friends to do right, to look out for themselves, to find honor in all of us looking out for each other.

I did call Dave back right away and cancel my order, then strongly suggested he find a better hustle. He wound up getting busted a few weeks later, probably snagging a ring for some guy who grew up to buy bootlegs of pirated videos for selling over the internet.

Although my enthusiasm for sporting the star-backed ring had waned, Bob insisted on taking me back to Kmart and buying it for me, no obligation. I volunteered to wash his car anyway, and not because it needed a scrub . . .

It was something I just needed to do.

WHAT WE LEAF

An Essay by
Stephen Geez
StephenGeez.com
Art by Dizzy

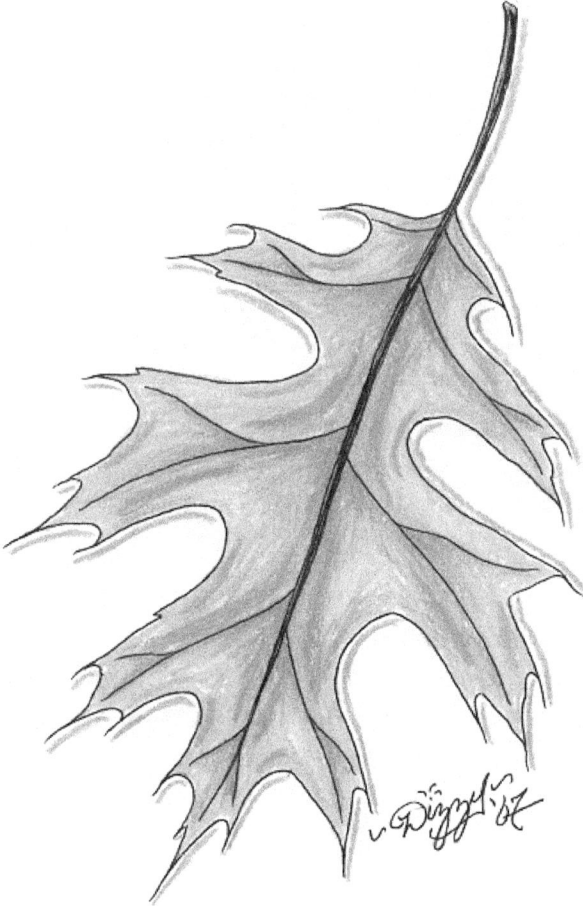

Comes a time all leaves ride the wind.

That's when many young'ns first take notice. They grow

fascinated by the simple, exquisite beauty in a single leaf. Many are driven to collect the prettiest ones, press a few between the pages of a book, even save them 'tween sheets of wax paper. Fascinated, they are, by the myriad shapes and sizes and colors, some appearing nearly perfect, all with tiny flaws that give them character, make them memorable.

In any vast tract of forest, you can find as many leaves as there are people in the world, all reaching for the light. You don't really see each one, though, as their differences blend into a canopy that shimmers and blurs in its vastness.

A scatter of leaves can remind us that, as with so many aspects of our world, it's worth a pause to look closer, to appreciate the splendor that passes through our lives.

To appreciate the people who pass through our lives.

You can't possibly see everybody in the crowd, but sometimes, when you're lucky, one or two will come close, and you'll notice. You'll see that simple, exquisite beauty in a lone soul. Then you might just spy another, even a few. We come in all shapes and sizes and colors, some nearly perfect, all with tiny flaws that give us character, make us memorable.

Whether you move through dense forest or the most crowded public square, you'll see countless individuals, each doing his job, working together to sustain the tree of life. You'll notice how we're tethered to our world, hanging on tight when the gales of adversity blow around and through us, tugging at what anchors us to purpose. And you'll discover that most of us do somehow manage to fulfill our destinies; but then toward the end, we begin to change, show our age, find our true colors, blaze brilliantly in those final moments before we must inevitably let go.

My fourth-grade class went on a leaf-collecting jaunt. Most of the children sought perfect specimens, one of each species to tick off a checklist. "Look! I've got a maple!" No need to look for any more . . .

Me, I searched for the odd ones, that maple with an ookie pattern of warty bumps, a sycamore boasting the crookedest lines, an oak teasing me with connect-the-dot pinpoint holes—leaves with attitude, as if they'd seen it all, had stories to tell. Most kids wanted the "pretty ones," but can we honestly dare to declare even the least one ugly?

All of us have tiny flaws that make us memorable.

So for now, you just keep on reaching for your own piece of the sun. Be proud of fulfilling your destiny. Remember to hang on tight when gales of adversity tug at your soul.

And don't be embarrassed when your age shows in the lines and bumps and colors that anyone who bothers to look can plainly see. Then cherish the opportunity to embrace your very own brilliant blaze of glory when it's your turn to let go.

Give the young'ns a reason to notice your simple, exquisite beauty—warts and all. Don't need wax paper, the pages of a book.

Comes a time all people ride the wind.

So live the wonder of a leaf.

Noted Kinfolk

BY SPECIAL ARRANGEMENT

An Essay by
Stephen Geez
StephenGeez.com
Art by Brian J. Smith

The world is in disarray.

But look closer, and you'll discover something extraordinary, a bright spot uniquely compelling, that most personal of expressions coaxing a hint of beauty.

Some are content to dwell within the chaos, while others can't help but impose order: a place for everything, everything in its place. What we need, though, are more of those rare individuals who see beyond the quotidian, the few who somehow intuit even the simplest ways to rearrange a small part of the world and thus touch our hearts.

My Aunt Dot is one.

Dorothy Stewart spends much of her time in that botanical delight she calls a backyard on the fringes of a byway in Middle Tennessee. By her very nature, if no longer by trade, she's a floral designer, master decorator, landscape artist, and quintessential arranger extraordinaire. Drop a few sprigs of fresh-cut this or that into any old soup can and she'll promptly create the most exquisite bouquet, a still life that refuses to sit still as it dares to come alive.

I've noticed two things about how Dot creates her magnificent arrangements: she works with whatever she's given, and she's willing to let go of that which does not fit.

Where another artist might strive to fulfill some precise, unwavering vision, sending you off to fetch that overly specific hard-to-find stem in the exacting shade of lavender, Aunt Dot instead looks closer until she discovers how to bring out the best in whatever waits patiently before her.

And where too many of us might never prove so bold, she'll not hesitate to chop that one shorter, strip a few of these leaves, peel one or two layers off that, and discard the rest of those. She'll declare that her world simply gets along better without all that, thank you very much.

Psychologists speak of the hierarchy of needs, the rudimentary understanding that we must necessarily focus first on food, shelter, our very *survival*; and that esthetics compete for attention only when our most primal necessities have been fulfilled.

But maybe all these needs really exist side by side, base survival and appreciation for beauty both engaged in a syncopated dance so one lifts us in time even as the other dips.

But what if we fall, or the world lays us out with the harshest of blows?

Many decades ago, as a young wife and mother, Aunt Dot faced a challenge greater than most could ever imagine. An instant of twisted metal and shattered glass left her critically injured, every new moment she managed to cling to life an unexpected miracle.

Is it possible at a time like that to seek beauty in a broken body? Maybe that's when it's most important to look ahead, to discover what might still come to pass, to summon the will to work with what we have and let go of that which no longer fits.

Where in any hierarchy of needs do we slot concerns about the size and shape of surgical scars? The stress of struggling to manage unmanageable pain? The fear of permanently losing one's mobility?—all the while knowing that five young children still need their mother, not so much for food and shelter, but for those profound expressions of love seen in helping a son match jacket with tie for his first formal date, in teaching a daughter how hair and makeup are but mere accents to highlight the beauty inside, in transforming the shelter of a family's house into the esthetics of a loving home.

We have faced many challenges in the years since, but Dot helps lift us by revealing beauty even as we struggle to survive tragedies that would pull us down.

Aunt Dot is legion, one of those wondrous souls who move quietly among us, a gentle touch here, a simple arrangement there, each showing us how much more they can't help but see.

They can't make everything right, and they know better than to try, but still they dance.

So let's appreciate the Aunt Dots in our lives, and let's strive to work with whatever lies before us, to let go of that which simply cannot fit.

Then look closer, and you'll discover something extraordinary, a bright spot uniquely compelling, the most personal of expressions coaxing a hint of beauty . . .

Even when your world's in disarray.

FULL THROTTLE

An Essay by
Stephen Geez
StephenGeez.com
Art by D.R. Wagner

Vrooom!

Full throttle, pedal to the metal!

Look out, Aunt Willene is fixin' to blow right by.

Aunt Willene is one of those, what you call, "senior citizens," a term that doesn't offend her sensibilities in the least.

She is one of many, a bubble of population boom squeezing its way through the narrow byways of our busy world. The number of seniors is mushrooming, their ratio to young people growing, our median age steadily rising. Aunt Willene is riding the front edge of that wave . . .

And she's cruising it on her ATV.

Yes, she's still tooling around town and zooming through the countryside on a souped-up 4-wheeler. Watch for her, and you'll see a prime example of one woman who refuses to slow down, especially when there's so much that still needs to be done.

Sure, she's been wrestling with many of the challenges that come from adding a few years to the old résumé, but then she got hit some time back by one of the big ones: a serious medical problem, the progressive kind you have to manage because there's no cure, one of those with its own foundation, stars raising money, an ad campaign to increase awareness. Her idea of a good day is one that's not as bad as the bad days.

Still, she works with Uncle Chester to manage the family farm, cares for bedridden kin, and somehow finds time to raise funds and support the local senior center, a project for which she's sold a bazillion of her trademark fried pies.

She especially likes to ride in the Christmas parade, the only time the police chief lets her show off without that hair-mussing helmet she hates so much to wear. She also collects impressive trophies from senior beauty pageants, her photo recently featured with other winners on a congratulatory billboard at the Waverly, Tennessee, city limits. So much recognition depends a lot, I suspect, on still looking as good inside as she does on the outside.

So why do some seniors tend to slow down while others like Aunt Willene keep the pedal to the metal—even when the path gets rough and that old engine's burning a lot more fuel these days?

Robert Frost used to ponder this, one of his more popular poems describing how it feels to stop by the woods one snowy evening, then remembering all those promises to keep, "miles to go before I sleep."

But maybe it's discovering, too often the hard way, that conquering each ever-steeper hill requires harnessing all that youthful momentum from the last one, that slowing down too much risks leaving one stranded with no place left to go.

Or maybe it's just about loving every precious moment of life, wanting to see what comes next, the exhilaration of slicing through stiff winds, dodging the deepest hazards, and barreling confidently down whatever trail stretches before us.

Whatever your reasons, remember that when you get to the point where your git-around isn't getting you around like it used to, it's time either to hit the gas or pull over and watch out because that next 4-wheeler to blow by just might be Aunt Willene.

Then think about getting on with living the way she does:

Full throttle.

Vrooom!

CREAM OF THE BOX

An Essay by
Stephen Geez
StephenGeez.com
Art by D.R. Wagner

Bob brought the donuts.

They usually proved quite tasty, too, but if you dive into boxes of fresh-baked cream donuts often enough, eventually you'll find some missing their filling. The icer's tank can hit a pocket of air or simply run dry, transforming the last few cakes into taunting false-advertisers sporting misleading holes in their sides . . . but no cream. Bob once unwittingly brought us a whole boxful of those brazen poseurs.

Aunt Doris and Uncle Bob Sullivan lived on the next street during my early years, a ubiquitous pair who never let a moment drag. After their jobs shifted to another state, they settled into a routine of making long drives to spend weekends with us, two families crowded into a small house—one big family, really, filling a home. Bob would rise early every morning and head out to brave the elements, returning with great heaps of warm pastries to rouse bleary-eyed sleepy-heads.

But then his trusty local baker betrayed him, reneging on the promise of gushy sweetness to squish with every bite. Pressed to explain, Bob just shrugged and told us, "I used a straw to suck out all the cream. Next time get up before I pull out my straw."

My little sister acted like she sort of believed him, and though Bob's threat became a running joke for many years, more than a few times I spied her pausing to inspect her selected confection for telltale signs of stealthy uncle tampering. That first bite filling her mouth with silky cream, she'd cast a sly glance his direction. Bob would narrow his beady eyes and say, "So I wasn't hungry . . . *this time.*"

As young donut-eaters move on to explore the bigger world, they inevitably cross paths with the sorts who *will* sneak the cream from another's lot, the ones who'll present a box of chocolates missing all the soft caramels, scrounge through a bowl of mixed nuts to claim their personal favorites, then pick through lettuce on a salad bar to pluck all the cherry tomatoes for themselves.

Still, these foibles are mostly harmless, but too often those same people become the movers and shakers who treat our world as their own personal salad bar. I'd prefer that timber barons understand the need to preserve at least some tracts of old growth, that builders would send wastewater downstream as clear as it flowed to them, that manufacturers prove willingness to move their own families to the very towns that breathe beneath the stacks.

But can't it be argued that you should seize the moment, enjoy every minute, take what you can and enjoy what you take? Why shy from the sunshine of a weekend with friends to save for lonesome rainy days? Why deny yourself a lifetime of creature comforts, only for the end to come in some dingy dive, your legacy a lumpy mattress stuffed with moldy cash?

Bob preferred, instead, his own brand of quiet selflessness. He'd buy all the fundraiser zoom-zooms to support my troop, surprise me with that new metronome my piano teacher advised, and take off work early to drive 200 miles so I could pick up my prom date in his new Cadillac.

It's that balance between self-interest and generosity of spirit that too many can't seem to strike, a rare feat Bob somehow managed to perfect. He could be an ornery, cantankerous curmudgeon who always made sure he got what he had coming, but he'd give it away in an instant if he suspected someone needed it more.

It's been decades since Uncle Bob died, far too young, much too soon. He did leave me some mementos, but his greatest gift was those weekends, countless moments that never dragged, cherished memories and the love that infused them.

As far as I know, Bob never actually ravaged any unwary donuts with his mischievous straw, but I'll never again eat a cream-filled pastry without checking for evidence that somehow he'd managed to get there before me.

And if I could find any way even now to let him take it, he'd be welcome to all the pastry fillings in the world.

Still, there's one thing too many people fail to remember:

It's easy to worry about who might want your share of the cream . . .

Just don't forget to appreciate whoever brings the donuts.

YOURSPACE

An Essay by
Stephen Geez
StephenGeez.com
Art by Dizzy

Most property owners mistakenly think they hold exclusive rights to a specified amount of space in a surveyed place, but where other two-leggers might agree not to tread, there lives a world of fauna not bound by the boundaries of man.

I'm talking about critters.

I'm talking not only about the bigger fellers such as mammals, but also your reptiles and amphibians, and don't even get me started on the plethora of birds and bugs out there. They'll watch, and they might even wait while you clear a plot, fence it off, and commence to build, but make no mistake: you're in their space, and soon they'll be in yours.

Aunt Mildred and Uncle JD retired some decades ago and headed for the hills of Alabama, there to set up a lovely homestead on a mostly cleared lot amid the old-growth timber of sugar maple, walnut, and stately pine. I'm sure their intrusion annoyed some of the local vermin. Most more likely eyed their efforts with a bemused eye for opportunity, especially when Mildred planted her garden, an effort she took quite seriously. She liked putting aside quality produce for sustaining family and friends during long cold Alabama winters.

Now, people generally enjoy living among wildlife, supporting conservation, minimizing disruption to the natural world. Many encourage a pleasant and friendly sharing of space, erecting houses and feeders and baths for birds, putting out salt licks and carrot/apple snacks for deer, submerging cover in adjacent waterways for fish, and of course leaving natural areas for groundhogs and all manner of, well, critters that live around and about.

Mildred has always enjoyed wildlife as much as anyone, but there in the hills she drew the line at her buildings and garden. Spiders were decidedly not welcome indoors, just as all things that spiders eat were considered more appropriately left outdoors. Rodents were advised to keep their distance. Birds were offered sufficient territory to nest away from the eaves, and anything interested in lingering in the garage found itself quickly and decisively dissuaded from such a notion.

Yet with all that gentle-but-firm nudging for squatting rights, none proved more entertaining than Aunt Mildred chasing varmints from her garden, especially rabbits and chipmunks—

ground squirrels, she calls the latter. Anybody observing while these hostilities escalated would have to think: This is going to get ugly . . .

And I'm talking about those fearsome rabbits with their guerrilla tactics.

While Aunt Mildred did achieve limited progress from time to time, we all know that's a losing battle, one where victories are measured in degrees of sustainable loss. Let's call it rent, extortion if you insist, palm-greasing for the locals who don't understand, let alone respect, man's folly of fence-lines and ownership.

But then the chipmunks made their move.

Aunt Mildred started having trouble with the family Ford losing power, so she took it in for service. The technician removed its air filter cover and found the compartment packed with hickory nuts. Yes, the chipmunks had co-opted Mildred's transportation as a place to put aside quality produce for sustaining chipmunk family and friends during long cold Alabama winters.

It's good when people find ways to share the world with the critters around them, but most would agree we have to draw the line at lending them a car.

So Mildred's Ford was put back in good working order, and while many might thereafter have been tempted to make futile attempts at sealing off the garage, she settled for monitoring and occasional hickory nut extraction as a means of ongoing discouragement. Until the day came that she moved northward to share space with one of her daughters and son-in-law, she kept a big bag of nuts in the back corner of the garage just in case, you know, somebody needed a bit of help sustaining family and friends during long cold Alabama winters.

Now Aunt Mildred enjoys living in the Tennessee hills, there on a wonderful spread with a sluice of rock-gouged stream running right out front. She likes to take walks along the water, but of course that's where an ornery mama-duck likes to nest.

I'd bet that quacker thinks she owns the place.

Yeah, this could get ugly.

A SIGHT FOR SORE EYES

An Essay by
Stephen Geez
StephenGeez.com
Art by Christopher Santino

Picture this:

It's a country scene, a spectacular day, and before you stands an old-fashioned grist mill, a long wall fronting the cool waters of a mill pond, its glassy surface rippled by a flotilla of languorous mill ducks, the shot framed by copses of regal, well . . . let's call them *mill* trees.

It's a postcard, a jigsaw puzzle, a brochure . . . it's Hurricane Mills—pronounced "hair-a-kin" if you want to sound like one of the locals. It's this serene and idyllic scene that Aunt Jean Buchanan has long enjoyed gazing upon, but there's more there than meets the eye.

Jean has long been a fixture working at the Loretta Lynn Ranch, a picturesque vacation destination in Middle Tennessee with campground, museum, the Butcher Holler homestead, Hurricane Creek canoeing and fishing, horseback riding, the antebellum plantation home shared by Loretta and her late husband, Mooney, the old mill house in the picture, and so much more.

Jean has been part of Loretta's team for—well, let's just say more than a few years. (Sometimes doing the math can be very impolite.) She likes to count herself among the Lynn family's friends, even having once lived with daughter Cissie Lynn for a while to help with Loretta's grandkids.

Jean loves this beautiful scenery and the myriad people who come from across the country and around the world to visit, so you can imagine our concern when she had to take an extended break from her time at the ranch. See, Jean began to suffer from an unusual vision problem, something about macular holes developing in both eyes, and suddenly she found herself nearly blind, unable to see her way around the world she knows and loves.

The notes she used to send me every few days stopped, no more cheerful cards saying, "We had 40,000 for Motocross this week—my ears are still ringing!" or one of her favorites: "Loretta is in town this week, doing a concert Saturday night—it'll be so nice to see her again."

Aunt Jean even had to hold off reading my latest book, and

she couldn't make her regular visits to my website to smile over my latest postings, maybe sending one with a message to a friend or two. Any writer knows that no matter how many eventually read your work, sometimes you find yourself staring at the keys thinking about saying something just for those few "fans" who matter the most.

Like Aunt Jean.

Jean agreed to undergo double surgeries. She knew the risks, on one hand possibly losing all her sight if the operations failed, on the other hand knowing she'd likely go blind anyway for trying to pretend nothing was wrong.

Luckily, the procedures seemed to go well, but for a time afterward she lived in a world of shadows and blurs. Still, she found herself recalling vivid images from a lifetime well lived: her children's first steps, crude drawings posted proudly on refrigerator doors, the fruits of successful gardens drooping heavily on the vines, the mail carrier bringing words from those who care. And she recalled the scenes of heartbreak, her niece and nephew taken too soon, friends facing challenges too great for any one body to endure, the dreams of those she loves accommodating the harsh realities of everyday life against the shifting backdrops of small-town life.

And she remembered the slow, wrenching loss of her husband, our beloved Uncle Van.

But even amid these heartbreaking visions she found images of truth, the contrasts of light against dark, and what she could see most clearly again was Uncle Van's gentle smile as he held his grandbabies tenderly, his face aglow, his heart soaring.

It was in those shadows and blurs of recovery that Aunt Jean dared face her own uncertain future. She looked ahead, best as she could see, and discovered that those grandsons of hers still could use an extra pair of eyes to watch over them, and the profusion of flowers arrayed across her porches and walkways still needed her tending, and the creek bank she always liked to stroll still waited with promises of birds to dance mid-air while hungry fish break the water's surface in search of fleeting willowflies, and her nephew still waited patiently for another of those notes—"Made some new friends today, and Loretta's back in town again"—those notes she always ended with the simplest of words, sometimes difficult to read, their meaning always clear as day: "We love you."

And the surgeries did succeed, giving Jean back her sight, at least for a time, a gift her latest note describes as "something we take for granted."

But, you know what? I don't think she ever takes anything for granted. See, Aunt Jean has always found immeasurable appreciation for that one small corner of the world she shares.

She doesn't work at the Loretta Lynn Ranch because she needs to, but rather because there she sees a vision of what we can all behold—if we're willing to look close. Even then, I believe she can see just a little bit more.

For it's in those moments, even when few are close by, that she can still see all those myriad faces from around the world; and though Mooney is passed on she can still see him in the legacy he left behind; and even when Loretta is off on a tour Aunt Jean can see the Lynn young'ns pursuing their own busy careers.

Even now, Jean can stand before that mill house and see the Lynn family there, generations sharing a wonderful bit of Middle Tennessee with those willing to make the journey . . .

And sharing it, too, with friends, old and young, even those who stop by from just up the road.

So picture this: it's a country scene, a spectacular day, and before you stands a magnificent old-fashioned grist mill, the cool waters rippled by a flotilla of languorous mill ducks who somehow seem simply to belong there.

And maybe Aunt Jean is nearby, maybe off to the side, or

maybe she's finally decided to retire and spend a bit more time looking after those boisterous grandsons of hers playing in the yard, or tending the profusion of magnificent flowers that line her porches and walkways, each an image committed forever to memory.

But like Loretta Lynn and her family, no matter how many generations come and go, a part of Aunt Jean Buchanan can always be found there at Hurricane Mills.

You might spot her if you're willing to learn the secret she carries deep in her heart:

Even in the darkest times, you can always remember the light, and you can always find another way to behold the most exquisite of scenes.

The trick lies in remembering also to picture those you love, the people who shared it with you.

Look close!

And remember: there's always more than meets the eye.

PUT A CHAIN ON IT

An Essay by
Stephen Geez
StephenGeez.com
Art by D.R. Wagner

Sometimes whenever my father is perplexed by a repair problem, people good-naturedly tease him by suggesting he "put a chain on it."

This dates way back to my high-school days in what they call one of those eras gone by. I'd purchased my first car which, owing to industry and parsimony, happened also to be a brand-new compact fresh off the assembly line. Soon I discovered that the vent lever, which normally shifts the fan-blower between heater and windshield defogger, had managed to lock up, thereafter refusing to budge.

Keep in mind, my father has always been able to fix anything. He's licensed in various skilled trades and, back in his career days, managed to keep an entire factory running, even sometimes in the face of daunting odds. Nearly everybody he knows has called him at one time or another with a problem only he could solve.

His concept of "fully functional" fits with the neat and orderly world he tries to sustain. He makes everything work, adapting whatever needs improvement, discarding what's no longer useful, even on occasion building something new if that's what will best do the trick. He's organized, with a place for everything and everything in its . . . Well, let's just say that we didn't accumulate much junk while growing up, since letting possessions slip below the radar of our attentions for too long risked later discovery that they'd been purged during one of my father's sweeps.

But more than a repair challenge, the vent lever clearly raised a bigger issue: safety. It threatened to endanger me on a dark road some cold night, leaving me unable to see where I drove.

My siblings and I always considered Dad a bit of a safety nut, a man infatuated with smoke detectors and motion sensors long before they came into fashion. If we stopped by for a visit, he'd invariably wander out to examine our tires, and having him over to our houses usually included an impromptu check of the furnace, or a "When's the last time you changed your . . .?"

We thought he tended to worry too much, but in retrospect it seems healthy doses of caution don't make for such a bad way to live. It's a dangerous world out there, one where sometimes just enough vigilance might prevent catastrophe or help avoid tragedy.

So after three trips to the dealership failed to increase the lever's reliability, my father decided to put a small chain on it. He attached it to the back of the mechanism, leaving it hanging from under the dash, then showed me how a simple pull on the chain whenever the lever froze up would solve the problem.

Everybody thought this was quite funny—but it worked. And though he's been teased about it ever since, his creative problem-solving has helped and protected a lot of people, if by no other means than devising some form of "chain" to do the job.

We all attach figurative chains to whatever we know will impact the lives of those we love, but we can't fix everything wrong with the world, nor can we squander our time trying too hard, and sometimes nothing we do can ever be enough. That's when in our grief we must find comfort in knowing we did the best we could.

Sometimes at dusk my father can be found on the porch, scanning the lake where he plans to catch a wily old bass, and he's content knowing the grass is mowed and the pilot lights are lit and the widgets all run smooth. His thoughts might wander to considering some new solution for an old problem, but there's no way he'll ever know how many ways he's truly helped so many people, the tragedies he's prevented, or at least the better nights of sleep he's given to those who know he's out there when they need him.

And though his own joys have been tempered by the most heart-rending of reasons to grieve, he always presses on, as do we all, a little wiser, always vigilant.

That vent-lever chain did wind up outlasting my first car, as I'm sure many of my father's "chains" inevitably will someday outlast him.

I've not met many people who would've been so determined to fix that nuisance device, nor who would consider it so important.

And my father's the only person I know who ever would have thought to put a chain on it.

Noted Traveling

COW IN THE CREEK

An Essay by
Stephen Geez
StephenGeez.com
Art by D.R. Wagner

When I convinced my friend Bill to accompany me on a raft/canoe trip through Alabama and Tennessee, never once did I imagine that he would nearly be eaten alive by a vicious cow.

Five days of torrential rains had swollen White Oak, one of the creeks where my father grew up fishing from holler to holler.

We planned to put in several miles east of Highway 13, expecting eventually to reach a Kentucky Lake boat landing beside the remnants of a decrepit washed-out bridge.

Uncle Calvin's car trouble and a lengthy detour conspired to put us hours behind schedule, but we set out, confident that rivers and creeks always promise one thing: Stay the course, regardless of obstacles and twists and turns, and you'll eventually get to where you're going.

The scenery looked spectacular, the sky vivid blue, the sun bathing us in its golden glow. We paddled enthusiastically, making up for lost time, but when the temperature hit something like 200 degrees, we discovered that Bill had brought the wrong float bag, the one packed with wetsuits for the next day's Ocoee rafting trip. We had no shorts or short-sleeve shirts.

We were in the middle of nowhere, and hadn't seen a soul, so if anybody did spot us that afternoon, now they know why two grown men decided to canoe in boxer shorts. Bill presented quite a sight, lobster-red due to his tendency to burn even at the mention of sunlight, a rather big guy who—well, he makes his end of the boat sit rather low in the water.

That's when we careened around a bend and spotted our adversary . . . a cow in the creek.

It was a calf, really, just standing there looking at us—two nearly naked nuisances paddling a canoe.

Frankly, I didn't think much of it, and we had plenty of room to maneuver around it, but Bill absolutely freaked. Apparently, the sum-total of his cow experiences had been to hang his head out car windows and Mooooo at indifferent herds. He didn't know that cows care more about the flies swarming their own rumps than about interlopers floating by in boats, or that their attention spans rarely last beyond the initial howdy-do.

So Bill panicked, paddled furiously, spun the boat around, and toppled us over. I found this rather annoying.

I managed to calm him down, then convinced him to risk life and limb by warily approaching the savage beast. The cow retaliated . . . by meandering up onto the gravel bar and waiting patiently for us to go away. Bill took a picture, proof of his brush with the most hideous of gruesome deaths.

As the air cooled, we dressed again, then found ourselves braving twisty rapids connecting deep crystalline pools that hosted lazy bass and curious bream. A Great Heron followed us for a while, and I tried to convince Bill it was planning to swoop down and peck out our eyes so the cows could move in and finish us off, but he didn't fall for it.

As the creek widened into deep floodwaters, we had to paddle hard to keep moving. I noticed that navigating our course had mimicked what it's like to live a long and full life: launched into the youthful swift-flowing currents of promise and potential, maneuvering around the obstacles and twists of fate, eventually slowing in the still waters of old age where even small progress requires extra effort.

We watched a glorious sunset, then found ourselves blanketed by a star-sequined shroud of impenetrable darkness, flashlights our only hope of surviving boat-eating trees. As the lake currents grew treacherous, the water choppy, Bill shared several colorful opinions about my skill at planning canoe trips, but we eventually found the decrepit old bridge, startling a young couple stargazing amid the rocks. As I stowed the gear, I could hear Bill regaling them with his tale of the deranged, bloodthirsty cow in the creek. I didn't hear it all, but I think he got to be the hero in his version.

If life is like a trip down a rain-swollen creek, then we better watch out for the cows. You might not consider them a threat, but one man's cow is another's fire-breathing Cow-zilla . . . and you never know which ones might be in cahoots with the Great Heron.

We drove to the Ocoee with barely enough time to stop for

breakfast. Bill ordered a thick steak with his eggs, and a big glass of milk.

I figured he'd already forgotten about the vicious cow that nearly ate him alive, but he did seem to take malevolent delight in carving his meat, chuckling to himself once or twice, grinning with every bite.

SKUNK SKOOL

An Essay by
Stephen Geez
StephenGeez.com
Art by Dizzy

What can we learn from a skunk?

And do you really want to get close enough to learn?

We all know any skunk encounter risks the potential for mal-odorous consequence, aroma therapy of the most aversive sort, the perfect example of how *not* having a dog's sense of smell can be a good thing.

I like watching those TV nature shows. Celebrated experts lead intrepid camera-toters to the far reaches for wildlife encounters, a chance to take us places most likely will never see for themselves, a wonderful way to learn about the critters who share our increasingly overlapping world. The better programs sneak in for a privy look. The worst barge in for a titillating daredevil encounter, preaching safety while teasing poison tentacles and snapping jaws just inches away: Look at me aren't I brave don't try this at home *I'm an expert!*

I've been known to induce friends to trek near and far for observatory encounters, not just with animals, but with the beauty of nature manifest in all its forms; so in this spirit many years ago I found myself driving with two urbanites to the farthest reaches of Michigan's Upper Peninsula for four days of camping, canoeing, hiking, and (not exactly the plan) feeding live human flesh to swarms of black flies on the Lake Superior shoreline.

We pitched tent as the only visitors at a rustic campground adjacent to a small lake nestled in old-growth forest, a short jaunt from the big water. Our first evening found us around the fire toasting marshmallows, the background an atavistic cacophony in SurroundSound from the blackness enclosing our flickering yellow corona, the urbanites having settled down after some initial apprehension about potential attack by marauding gangs of snakes or bobcats or bears or worse.

That's when the 'coon showed up.

She appeared at the far end of the circle of sites, then methodically worked her way around, checking trash barrels, smelling fire rings, and scavenging the fringes where grass ceded its buffer to dense woods. She skirted our area, careful to keep some distance, yet eyeballing everything, confirming potential after-fire largess with some highly targeted sniffing. Assured that raccoons are never known to pounce upon humans and gnaw about their noses and ears, my friends watched, enthralled, rapt, amazed, and generally fascinated by so mundane an encounter.

Still, it was cool.

Better yet, having ascertained the lack of danger, our 'coon disappeared for a moment, then returned with two tiny coonlets and commenced supervising while they performed their own inspection. My friends quietly debated how "natural" this behavior was, finally agreeing with me that it's as natural as teaching any youngster how to thrive in whatever environment he finds himself.

Long after the raccoons had moved on, the midnight shift came aboard: one large skunk. Yes, a white-striper, Pepe LePew without the French accent, a mega-stinker.

He worked the far side of the campground, then headed straight for our site, seemingly uncowed by the presence of people, the two-legged species that, presumably, had never proven aggressive in all his skunkly experience. My friends fled to the car. Wimps. Skunks don't jump on people, either.

So I sat on the picnic table and watched as he examined our property, his nose eventually pointing toward the food stacked right where I was practicing my skills at being very still. He inched closer, then placed his paws on the bench and proceeded to sniff my shoes and legs. I could hear my friends in the car some hundred feet away freaking out behind sealed windows and locked doors—their assumption being that skunks don't carry master car keys. That's when the most wonderful act of friendship occurred, my buddies transcending their own fears to put my well-being ahead of all else:

The jokers started honking the horn and flashing the headlights to startle the skunk.

Ha ha ha. Oh, *Wouldn't that be a hoot?* they must have thought, apparently not thinking far enough ahead to imagine sharing a tent or car-ride home with a hapless soul who had been, well, skunked.

But I knew better, and so did the skunk. Bearing no malice toward me, and finding no threat in them, he ignored the goofballs.

Instead, he eyed the food, and I knew this encounter wouldn't end until he enjoyed a snack. Now, I normally discourage feeding wildlife, but this four-legger had already made the campground part of his circuit, and he was already comfortable with humans without posing any real bodily danger, so I casually placed four graham crackers on the bench in deference to a situation over which I had little control. He made four quick trips to carry them into the woods, then came back, stopped before the table, and looked at me as if to say thanks. He turned to look toward the pranksters, who had finally settled down, their faces pressed against the glass. I swear in my head I could hear the skunk asking, "So what should we do about *them?*" I wanted to hand him the keys and tell him go have some fun, but he had nightly rounds to finish, and I'm pretty sure they would keep relocking the door before he could get it open.

So he disappeared into the woods. Figuring he would make another round after we'd crashed, I left a slice of bread out, which was gone in the morning. He did return at the same time every night, and my friends retreated to the car every time, both sides of that detente being something I enjoyed watching.

A bit short of sufficient material for an hour-long documentary, this encounter still begs the question: What can we learn from a skunk?

This funny feller boasted quite a weapon, and my friends proved quite wary of it. Still, their behavior showed that they wrongly assumed it likely to be used for offense. It seems this difference of perspective is one that impacts global geo-politics rather poignantly. Skunks do have a rather distinctive defense, but they are not known for initiating pre-emptive strikes. It takes actual injury or genuine fear for a skunk to unleash its scent. While it is good to know approximately where that threat-threshold lies, deliberately provoking him was not likely the best way to build a foundation for future anthropo-skunk relations. If our mere oc-cupation of his world had come to mean presumption of attack, his understandable use of defensive capabilities would have en-couraged us to assume he might well attack us first. Gosh, that kind of scenario could spiral out of control.

And make it difficult ever to put the balance back where it belongs.

Another lesson we might note is how the skunk never lost sight of his own mission. Provoked by interlopers, he proved sharp enough to understand that I was not in cahoots with the enemy. Had they cornered him, he surely would have unleashed, but he harbored no animosity toward me, purported no alleged link borne of expedience or politics, had no constituency to ap-pease.

It's good that skunks reserve such powerful chemical weapons to protect themselves. Within the forest there lurk many dangers, so natural selection gave rise to this uniquely effective survival strategy. Knowing our skunk's mere willingness to use it became our deterrent. Counting on his measured reluctance became the basis for him and me to develop a rudimentary trust, to share a campsite in his neck of the woods.

I'd like to say we all became buds, he and my friends warming up to each other, the four of us sitting around the fire toasting marshmallows and regaling ourselves with scary stories of woods-prowling monsters: axe murderers, slimy mutants, flesh-eating flies, and the dreaded (shiver!) perfume-manufacturer sales rep. But no, the skunk stuck to his own plan while we stuck to ours, which after all had brought us here to cross paths with nature, to engage some informative encounters with the wild, to simply ob-serve critters doing their critterly thing in our critter-filled world.

So, can we learn anything from a skunk?

WAYS OUT

An Essay by
Stephen Geez
StephenGeez.com
Art by Dizzy

Do you have a sound exit strategy?

I hope you have at least one. If not, maybe it's time you start planning. You can never have too many.

It's an awful feeling, suddenly finding yourself trapped. We've all felt it to varying degrees at various times as we voraciously live our variable lives. Sometimes we can see it coming; sometimes it'll catch us by surprise.

We take comfort in knowing that somehow we usually manage to extricate ourselves, no big deal, but there inevitably comes a time when the stakes are high, options dangerously limited, precious time ticking away. That's when having gone in with a sound exit strategy can prove priceless.

I once joined my scuba-buddy Bill exploring the reefs off Cozumel, Mexico. Late in a dive at Kent's Caves, he grew curious about some activity inside a sandy-bottomed coral underpass in water more than a hundred feet deep. Pursuing a better look, he wriggled head-first into a space barely big enough to accommodate him, leaving me with the rather less-than-scenic view of a reef that appeared embarrassed about its unnatural protuberance of hairy calves and rubber fins.

Several beats passed. Then Bill tried to back his way out.

And got stuck.

Now, in scuba-diver parlance, people who do this are referred to in technical terms ranging from "knucklehead" to "victim" or "drowning fatality."

Scuba exploration is one of those activities during which simple miscalculations are quickly compounded. In a crisis at depth, the stakes are high, options dangerously limited, precious time ticking away. At most, his tank offered five minutes of air, and he would need at least four of that to ascend and decompress before reaching the surface.

He clearly had not expected to find himself so unceremoniously stuck. Otherwise, he might not have gone in, or at least he would have planned better. He could have first swept out some of the sand to enlarge the opening. At minimum, he might have cleared the other side to provide an alternate exit. He should have kept one hand in reach of his BC release in case he needed to slip temporarily out of his gear.

To his credit, though, he did go in with the best backup plan of all:

A buddy.

Smart divers never dive alone. They work as a team, monitor each other, and always stand—fly, climb, swim—ready to assist. He never would have descended to that depth, let alone risked wedging himself into a crevice, if not for the presence of his (smart, charismatic, and resourceful) friend.

Noting how his movements grew uncharacteristically frantic, I swam close enough to grip his leg, a signal of calming reassurance. He relaxed enough for me to shift his body for a better look. I could see light ahead, but not enough space for him to work through. I tested moving him several ways and discovered his tank had become lodged in a crevice. I had to push him in deeper to dislodge it. Once I gently eased him free, he signaled the okay, and we headed for the surface.

I think an elaborate thank-you dance on the dive boat would have been nice, but I didn't object when he offered to pay for dinner that night.

You don't have to be underwater to find yourself trapped. Maybe you're buried in debt, or you want out of a relationship that is proving unhealthy. Your transportation can break down, and suddenly you're mired in snow or sweeping away in the flood. Maybe someday you'll find yourself overimbibed, with no designated driver; or far from home, your wallet lost or stolen.

Have you charted your escape route in case of fire? Do you keep basic repair and survival kits in your car? Do you plan every adventure with contingencies for worst-case scenarios?

Whether the goal is to have more fun or simply endure an ordeal without panic, preparedness brings peace of mind. It's a lot easier to slide into the stifling confines of an MRI machine if you're holding the panic button, knowledge that you do have a fast, sure way out.

Even if you never have to use it.

Preparedness includes anticipating potential changes in perspective. That vertiginous view from the summit can prove surprisingly scary, but don't forget that if you found a way to climb up, that means there must be a way down. Have the foresight to anticipate your controlled descent; then let your plan trump your fear.

Sometimes you can be trapped and not even know it. The right buddy is someone you trust to clue you in, but you must be willing to listen.

Sometimes you can feel trapped simply because you don't see the way out. The right buddy offers a signal of calming reassurance, but you must be ready to trust.

When you're looking for light at the end of the tunnel, a buddy doesn't just have your back . . .

A buddy brings the map.

But *you* need to plan ahead, too, because your buddy is also depending on you.

Don't stop peering into caves, climbing peaks, probing depths. Those are some of the best ways to discover what life is all about. But always think twice before you venture in.

And have a sound exit strategy.

WEBSTERS' WORLD

An Essay by
Stephen Geez
StephenGeez.com
Art by Dizzy

Gossamer threads undulate languidly in the morning breeze. Silken funnels crouch in shadowy afternoon corners. Geometric constructs dreamcatch the inviting gaps in foliage, backlit by silver-gold bursts of setting sun. Spiders lurk about, nature's constructors transforming the world.

If you're lucky enough to live where seasons proclaim their changes, you might recognize springtime by its burgeoning effusions of flora: trees budding, perennials sprouting, grasses greening. Or maybe you note the songs: birds serenading, frogs counterpointing, crickets syncopating time. Me, I've always looked for less-obvious signs, the commencement of building: cracks growing anthills, eaves sprouting birds' nests, nooks and crannies boasting new spiderwebs.

Spiders know what they're doing when it comes to harnessing the potential of their own unique thread-producing talent. They cast like fly-fishermen, parachute their young, doggy-bag tonight's snack, trap watery bubbles, and decorate from cityscape to countryside, inside and out. I've even heard of one writing "SOME PIG" for its friend Wilbur, but that might be fiction.

Spiders are quite different from people. They're not meant to share our space, and generally not welcome in close quarters—except that we begrudge them our gardens to feast on bugs that would otherwise devour our food.

Confronted by a spider at close range, many people tend to react viscerally. No wonder: spiders are hairy little critters that appear bigger than life. They clearly pose a mortal threat, and often display the brand of malevolent intent found in serial killers—or worse. Hence, spiders serve as ideal fodder for Halloween scarefests, horror flicks, and the kinds of practical jokes that jokesters learn never to repeat.

Spiders have elicited worship, sacrifice, and more than a few myths and legends, some of which I brazenly co-opted to spin the tale in my novel *The Fixer: Spider-Boxed*. I think there's even a comic-book/movie hero having to do with super spidey powers. Bad guys, beware!

Sure, some spiders can be poisonous, dangerously so, but those species are rare and few, and instances of people-gnawing tend to classify as spider self-defense. Most of the bad rap for "spider bites" is unearned. More often the culprit proves some other biter, or maybe even a scratch, any damage from subsequent infection by a bacterial strain, likely staph, possibly an antibiotic-resistant superbug known as MRSA. For spiders wrongly accused, there is no Innocence Project to seek justice.

Actually, spiders really are quite vulnerable. Except for a few notable exceptions, most appear very small. None enjoy the hard-shell protection or vice-grip pincer defense of their crab cousins, or the poisonous slingblade whiptails of their other cousins, the scorpions. Watch even a big spider tangle with a wasp; the sure money bet is backing that wiry combatant with a stinger in his tail. Of course, a tarantula can shoot itchy hairs at you. Big whoop.

I've always admired the spider's ability to weave webs. A great wonder of nature, spider silk embodies properties science and engineering are only beginning to understand and harness. Still, the remarkable variety of webs produced by various species seem miraculous in themselves, testament to niche adaptation—not to mention a good way for the spider-wary to monitor the location of any eight-legged adversaries.

Okay, I admit it: I'm spider-averse, too. As one known all my life for a fascination with—and propensity to handle—all manner of creatures, I harbor an uncharacteristically deep reluctance to share personal space with any spider of any size.

And I sure don't want one on me.

My worst spider nightmare occurred decades ago in the Everglades. Two friends and I crowded into a tiny, leaky, miserable excuse for a wooden skiff, its petulant 3-horsepower motor near-worthless even when it occasionally puttered along between stallings. Miles into backwater swamps, we found ourselves in the dim wash-channels of thickening trees and brush while the purple sky darkened with great roiling storm-clouds.

We had ventured into the lair of Florida's spider-beast, the great Golden Orb.

Yes, everywhere we looked, massive six- and eight- and ten-foot webs gated the escape routes. Though photographically exquisite in their symmetry, up close in person they proved threateningly ominous. Worse, their centers boasted monstrous black-and-gold spiders the size of a man's finger-spread hand.

The boat motor chuckled a few times at our predicament, then sputtered and died. Rick yanked feverishly on the cord while Scott and I worked against each other and the rising wind, churning muck with splintery wooden paddles. Suddenly the motor caught a spark and roared to life. We were saved!—except Rick hadn't disengaged it, so the boat lurched forward, ramming us right through the brush and webs, leaving us lodged deep in one of Dante's levels of arachnid hell.

Spiders rained down on us, flailing about the boat, crawling on our bodies, their silken strait-jackets wrapping us ever tighter—

Well, if you've ever unexpectedly walked your face through a web, you know the feeling.

Of course we eventually managed to escape unscathed, and now it all seems rather amusing. I mean, what felt like an attack on us must have felt to them like *our* aggression. We'd blundered our way into *their* homes and hunting grounds, destroying a day's web-work, costing them each an all-important chance to earn their sustenance. I'm sure the spiders harbored no grudge, though. They simply rebuilt, just as people do after catastrophes.

So next time you spot a chilly-morning web outlined by beads of glistening dewdrops, remember to think past the creepy-crawlies, and admire the sheer wonder of nature's glory.

Spiders always find a way. Spiders always find a place.

Maybe we're not so different after all.

I'm admiring the work of a spider right now—but no, I don't need to look closer, thank you very much. I mean it. Let's not disturb the hairy littler critter . . .

SOOPER-DAWGING

An Essay by
Stephen Geez
StephenGeez.com
Art by Dizzy

Always one of the adventurous types, I've generally classified my
cohorts as either Sooper Dawgs or Fraidy Cats—not that either

trait is more virtuous than the other—but there are many grades between the two, and in myself I always preferred to cultivate a healthy streak of both.

I can cite examples of Sooper Dawg friends, the kind who are first in or up or under or over the edge, but I've also witnessed two examples from the pet world who appeared to fit the moniker, in both cases literally real dogs. The first appeared with his young-man companion while I was hiking and climbing a series of red-rock ridges in Arizona, not the kind of route that required equipment, but one that presented off-trail options for some precarious thrills and spectacular views accessible even to an impressively deft-footed pooch. The other led a young couple past me while I hiked a cliff-face ledge to a sitting spot overhanging the ocean, a promontory extending from the Pacific Coast Highway south of Big Sur.

In both cases, the quasi-path ended at a protruding dome rock, a billiard-ball-smooth jut thrusting its way outward and upward. These locations shared two common characteristics. First, the shape meant that standing on top would seem fairly easy, but getting up the steep side—and this is the important part—then back down safely would be difficult. Second, a deal-breaker, the consequences of a slip would inevitably prove fatal. Below the coastal dome a two-hundred-foot drop would dash me on jagged boulders so crashing waves could move in to lift my body gleefully for a game of "toss the idiot rag-doll." Below the Arizona dome a steep, gravelly slope afforded no way to stop catapulting for at least a thousand feet before an unceremonious bounce against the wall of a deep dry gulch. I found no appeal in the notion of trying either.

In both situations, humans did let common sense prevail, but the dogs failed to understand that a trail can and sometimes should, well, end before it ends. Against their owners' futile entreaties, both bounded upwards, slipping and sliding until they achieved the pinnacle, there to stand gazing raptly across the horizon, a moment of exuberance before slipping and sliding back down to be caught in the arms of relieved masters.

Here's the trick: In neither case did the dogs ever look down. They didn't realize the danger, never considered the hazards, hadn't weighed the risks against such a minor reward.

Me, I always look down. Then I make a calculated assessment and consider multiple contingency plans. Without at least one good escape hatch, my untested rocket's not likely to leave the pad. I've always played Sooper Dawg like a Fraidy Cat.

I can tell you stories, and maybe someday I will, but suffice it to say that when trapped floating in total darkness, pulled by an overpowering current miles off the coast of Venezuela, I swear my scuba buddy and I had already confirmed where the flow would take us if we couldn't return to the entry point, leaving us shining dim flashlights at waves battering hundred-foot Bonaire cliffs until hours later we'd eventually sweep into the leeward bay, a simple swim to the resort beaches and Commercial Pier. And you can bet that prior to that we'd devoted countless hours to extensive training for handling all manner of scuba emergencies, every dive requiring Plans B and C and then some. No, homey don't parachute without a reserve.

It's also critical to know what to expect. The savvy rafter who's run the same stretch a hundred times knows that first trip down after floodwaters have rearranged the river's rocks requires stopping before every rapids to scout the route on foot.

Still, in all the wild situations I've found myself, I always felt confident I could keep my wits and find the best option for preserving my safety, but I've long understood that I do have one internal impediment that might rise momentarily in one specific kind of situation: hints of vertigo at extreme heights.

I discovered this as a wee lad when I climbed atop the house and got too scared to climb back down, having to rely on my father to bring a ladder. The opinion he expressed about getting myself into such a predicament surprised me: Instead of saying I simply shouldn't climb up on the house, he warned that I shouldn't be climbing anyplace from which I'm not completely sure I can get myself back down. I hadn't thought about that before my glorious ascent, and neither had those canines bounding up onto the slippery domes.

Getting out of bed is a calculated risk. Leaving the house, driving a car, using an ATM . . . these can be just as dangerous as any smartly planned wilderness adventure, but nowhere near as exhilarating.

Some people find thrills in danger, but I posit that keeping it safe allows us to experience even greater thrills. If I ever fly off the trapeze, I'll enjoy it more knowing there's a net, and likely fly higher and stretch farther if I'm confident I can afford the flash.

What I won't do is fly blind on a route no one I trust has scouted. The people to avoid are those who act like dome-climbing dogs, the ones who don't have sense enough to look down.

Life can be an adventure if you approach it right.

I say, approach it like a Fraidy Cat, and you too can live the exciting life of a Sooper Dawg.

SCRATCH-BACK

An Essay by
Stephen Geez
StephenGeez.com
Art by Dizzy

Fish actually waited in line to enjoy a day of pampering at the fish spa, premium package, all amenities included. A classic case of win-win, getting along is so much easier when everybody has something to gain.

I discovered this odd mix of strange bedfellows during a trip to Bonaire of the Netherlands Antilles, off the coast of Venezuela. I'm not mixing metaphors by calling them "bedfellows," either, because I am referring to denizens of the ocean bed—an area of sloping reef, specifically, where the shallows offer last refuge along the coral fringe above yawning deep. Scuba-diving with a friend, I happened upon a scenario I'd never encountered and had not yet learned about. There among the sea-fans and tube sponges, I found a line of six or eight variously affiliated fishes, literally lined up, their engines idling, waiting for a turn at what I now know marine biologists call a "cleaning station."

As each fish moved to the front of the queue, it would ease into a shallow depression that appeared to have been fanned out. Scores of tiny shrimp and other myriad critters I could never identify would swarm the scaly client and proceed to clean it. The fish would hold its mouth open, splay its gills, still its fins, and otherwise settle in for its private session at the spa. The attendants would move quickly, scouring parasites, algae, slime, dead cells—anything the fish could live healthier without, and which offered the crew a free meal, or at least the satisfaction of a job well done, gratuity not included.

Most amazing about this spectacle was watching these critters clean *inside* the fishy mouths when just minutes before—and presumably minutes after—those fish wouldn't hesitate to eat the little groomers, as well as their siblings, cousins, and any friends.

The fish dare not disrupt this age-old dance of the mutual back-scratch because they need these services to enhance their ability to survive, not to mention how much better parasite eradication must make them feel. The shrimps and their cohorts, enjoying home delivery in an umpteen-course ready-to-eat meal, have learned not to fear being eaten because they know their clients both want and need the good cleaning.

Back home, I did some research and learned a lot about these cleaning stations, including other examples in both saltwater and freshwater environments. Land-based critters enjoy many versions, as well, my favorite being the cleaning services several species of birds offer mammals such as rhinos. It's quite a sight, those delicate little assemblages of feathers and beaks cleaning the teeth of a giant muck-wallower dutifully holding its mouth open as if the dentist had instructed, "Say aaaah."

Comparisons come easily, the image of those fish lined up for service rather like cars awaiting a premium-package car wash and detailing. The dentist image works well, too, as do other bodily variations including the combo massage, wax, and mani-pedi. I could go on, but one common theme is that human teams providing services derive their benefits primarily in the form of monetary payment. Granted, this is how we operate, trading in the currency of symbolic units to represent expended effort and other non-specific goods.

Many smart people have used this model of mutual benefit quite elegantly. It's a lesson many sharp businesspeople have taken to heart.

Expand your fast-food chain into a minority-dominated enclave and you might earn some modest profits as an outsider bringing in outside employees to trade product for a small piece of the neighborhood economy, but you'll do much better if you make your enterprise part of the local landscape, hiring locally to bring in job opportunities as much as you take profits out. Smarter yet, offer franchising opportunities, and facilitate everything from training to financing so locals will own a place on your team, even as you become part of the local community. The benefits to both sides of that equation will grow exponentially, including much greater support from the customer base you hope to tap.

Consider how car companies from outside the USA carved out such a huge portion of the customer base. What began as a fractional niche market of imports has grown into a vast industry woven into the economies of entire regions, ranging from using local suppliers, to staffing factories with local labor, to conducting R&D in centers close to the people being asked to support those products with their dollars.

Long before currency came to dominate transactions, barter encouraged people to discover new ways work together, whether it be trading inventory, waste, services, or expertise. There is no limit to the myriad ways these alliances play out today, but I like to think we could do more.

I am especially fond of the notion that people who are very different from each other—people who might never get along any better than big fish and tiny shrimps on open reef—not only can find ways to help each other achieve rewards neither could hope to achieve alone, but also can increase understanding and harmony among individuals, communities, congregations, or even nations.

A young couple moves into a starter house, maybe needing some wisdom and assistance from the retired carpenter next door, the older coot with the bad hip who is having a lot of trouble keeping his lawn mowed . . .

Maybe the teen who is a wiz at developing 'net applications could use some mentoring in business-planning from the local entrepreneur who is ready to learn more about expanding her enterprise to the 'net.

Parents have been swapping childcare for ages, but maybe it's time to look more toward swapping for skills training, hands-on career experience, even recreational opportunities to relieve the pressure.

Older people have a lot of skills and knowledge they can share, but so do the young. If you want to reach out to other communities, or ethnic groups, other religious faiths, people who live very differently than you, seek out new ways to forge new alliances where both parties benefit. Don't write off the gangs, the prisoners, the poor, the infirm, the people who don't speak your language, those who don't see the world exactly like you.

You might expand your world view, see life through the prism of everyman. You might come out way ahead of the old pay-as-you-go model. You might learn to trust others, and to discover that the more we need each other, the more we look out for each other.

Even fish and tiny shrimps can figure out that much.

Getting along is so much easier when everybody has something to gain.

DON'T LEAP BEFORE THEY LOOK

An Essay by
Stephen Geez
StephenGeez.com
Art by Dizzy

Anybody who achieves his every goal probably isn't aiming very high, yet the higher we aim, the more people might notice if we happen to fail.

My friend Bill once found himself aiming rather high even as he gazed straight down. He stood teetering at the edge, there atop the world, high above the waters at the westernmost tip of Jamaica.

Still young and relatively unobligated, Bill and I rented a vacation condo on the beach at Negril back in the days before untrampled sands and dense jungle yielded to a clutter of hotels and all-inclusive resorts. We knew we'd found paradise when our dreadlocked host greeted us by broom-shooing giant crabs from the lobby, a poignant welcome to kick off a week of jerk grilling, mango chilling, lobster boiling, and Red Stripe swilling.

Our first evening found us lounging at the shoreline, overrun by marauding crustaceans, admiring that spectacular light show known thereabouts as "sunset." A noisesome boatload steamed by, several dozen revelers trekking toward a private islet for the nightly clothing-optional party, bonfire, and barbecue. A couple of the lovelier ladies on deck smiled our way and waved before disappearing into a blinding parfait of shimmering cloud-layered light.

Bill was a big fellow, his round white belly in need of some Jamaican tan, but he never shied from physically challenging adventures. Chattering enthusiastically about our plans to climb waterfalls, raft mountain streams, and snorkel coral gardens, he suggested we also explore the point's picturesque limestone cliffs, then swim the eddies, washouts, and surf-carved caves below.

Imagine our excitement the next afternoon when we discovered an exquisite inlet with deep crystal-clear water pooling below a towering overhang, the perfect high-board for brave divers still young and relatively unobligated. We stashed our gear and methodically climbed the precipice, then immediately noted that simple truism known to all similarly situated: It always seems way higher looking down from the top than it does looking up from below.

Pretending to linger for enjoying the view, we reminded ourselves that we'd already confirmed sufficient water depth for any manner of plummet. Still, we agreed that our intentions all along had been merely to jump, the notion of swan-diving best left to trained professionals. He maintains that we also agreed I would go first, but I'd have to read back the minutes to see exactly who made that motion and how it managed to garner majority votes with a quorum of only two.

Now, I've jumped out of a few airplanes in my time, and once even found myself bungee-jumping from a hot-air balloon in the foothills of the Rockies, so I know that when it's time to go, the patience of others waiting a turn quickly wears thin. If you're going to leap, you might as well just go ahead and, you know, *leap*.

So I, um, lingered a bit longer to, you know, enjoy the view some more, then eventually grew impatient with myself and simply took the plunge.

You should have seen me. Imagine a ballet in mid-air, somersaulting gracefully, soaring like a majestic eagle, shifting my body to form the letters spelling my name, acting out a brief scene from *Hamlet*, even swapping birdly stories with a few gulls who swooped in to join me.

Then picture what really happened, which looked more like a flailing crash-test dummy striving to stay right-side up lest the inevitable smack sting more places than even the Jamaican sun might shine. Yes, it did prove exhilarating, but not in a do-it-again sort of way.

Then I looked up, squinting against the glare, and noticed Bill peering over the edge, the very picture of cautious appraisal framed by the reckless abandon of boundless blue sky. Problem was, five and then ten and more minutes later, he was still up there, by which time I'd grown bored with treading water. At one point we exchanged shouts about the notion of him climbing down, but the route up had proved fairly challenging, so any unceremonious retreat would likely engender even greater risk, certainly more than simply dropping into the welcoming embrace of our Jamaican water mistress.

So I took to offering him words of encouragement, the kind that come out more like "Hey, man, jump! Just do it! Jump!" Waving my arms and gesturing impatient hurry-downs punctuated my pitch with supporting visuals.

Then we heard that familiar chug-chug, and the daily islet boat-run appeared around the jut, loaded down with its customary eruption of raucous partiers swilling Red Stripes and capering about in anticipation of an ever more Bohemian night. Somebody spotted Bill atop the cliff, so the boat made a fast turn and steamed right up alongside the small cove, then reversed engines for a full-stop and cut the power. Our flirty ladies appeared topside as revelers swarmed this end of the deck, more climbing the bridge, the impromptu observation post listing precariously as the crowd started chanting "Jump! Jump! Jump! *Jump!*"

While I would never advocate overriding one's righteous sense of self-preservation simply to satisfy the goading of a spirited mob, I have to admit I wouldn't want to be the one seen running scared by the very group we'd talked about joining at the bonfire some subsequent evening. So there Bill stood like the proverbial jumper on a ledge, the crowd demanding its show. He summoned the courage, steeled his resolve, and stepped into the breath-stealing void.

It really was a beautiful sight, and I'll confess now after all these years that I was fibbing when I told him I could hear a small thunderclap from air rushing back to fill the swath cut by his trajectory. He hit the water hard, sank like an anvil, kicked feverishly, and surfaced in triumph.

And the crowd went wild.

They screamed, whooped, hugged each other, toasted his success, poured beer over each other's heads, then grabbed fast handholds as the boat powered up and chugged out of the cove. They would continue celebrating on their topical islet, spinning and re-spinning the story, the legend of that white-bellied cliff-diver growing more impressive with every telling.

Life can be full of little victories, and those are usually tempered by the occasional failures, but it's the bad habit of give-ups that can discourage us most, especially when we keep our goals secret so nobody finds out we never even dared try.

I do hope you all remember to encourage the people in your world. Whether it's for accomplishing something important or merely seeking a bit of fun, you might help make the difference, and you might just get a little bit of that back-patting back.

And try not to give up on your own wanna-do's before you at least check the depth and climb to the summit for an honest look-see.

Tell the world, then steel yourself and give it a try.

So here's to hoping the next time *you* take a leap of faith, you have your own raucous boatload of supporters gathering to cheer you on.

Noted Around Me

CONSTANT MOON

An Essay by
Stephen Geez
StephenGeez.com
Art by Dizzy

Was a time not too awfully long ago I sat with my lady-friend on a romantic velvet-sky night and admired the splendor of the full moon. Reminded of how that experience still moved us years later, she suggested I write an essay about our planet's sole lunar companion.

As if to assert I can, would, have, and often do write on just about any mundane topic, I promised someday I would get around to it. Eventually I asked Fresh Ink Group artist Dizzy if he would render me his vision of a full moon, something conveying notions of majesty and omniscience, and most certainly—at which Dizzy's depictions excel—something with a bit of, you know, attitude. He did, and I promptly filed and forgot about it.

Until now!

Last night the moon caught my eye. It seemed to have an attitude, so after waiting too long, I'm now writing about the moon; and as if to prove I can, would, have, and often do write about things that aren't really what I'm writing about, I'm going to make the true subject of this essay more obvious than usual. I'm about to compare the moon to one's lifelong partner/spouse/lover/ friend.

Now, everybody who can see has seen the moon. We've all been aware of it since at least our younger days when somebody clutching a book of nursery rhymes yammered at us about a cow jumping over it.

We've been told, also likely in those early years, that the moon is made of cheese—*green* cheese, specifically—and maybe for a time we even bought that kind of malarkey. Legend has it that a lot of auld-days moon-gazers truly did believe it, and given many people's patently prevalent propensity to perpetuate ancient myths at the expense of modern science, I'm sure a national poll would turn up at least a significant percentage of adherents who still assert the cheese explanation.

It has even been said that the moon's influence can encourage a soul to do crazy things, to engage in the behavior of, well, a luna-tic. Heck, what's a bit of benign lunacy between loony soulmates?

What we know of the moon is that it's quite a big chunk of elemental matter. As hypotheses are painstakingly tested until they become overwhelmingly supported theories, it appears that luna most likely originated from a cataclysmic event that broke it off from what would eventually become our own orbiting world: terra—Earth, if you will. Though an entity of its own now, the moon is still a part of us, exerting a constant pull on our world, on our bodies, and even on our psyches.

Pretty much like that exquisite soul who loves you most, who is and always will be a part of you.

This is someone we feel, the one who exerts a pull on us. Can one truly love and not be lowered by a loved one's pain, or lifted by the elations of the one we cherish?

Children are awed by how the moon seems to follow them around. Watch out the car window on a long night drive, and gosh durn it if that ol' buddy isn't right out there following along, making every turn, keeping an eye out, enjoying the journey, sharing the ups and downs.

Study a full moon near the horizon, maybe hanging just above some buildings, and it looks substantially bigger than it will later as it rises higher in the sky. Many assume this is caused by atmospheric distortion, but the biggest factor is optical illusion, entirely in the mind, perception as a matter of mental perspective. It's affected by proximity, comparative objects appearing nearby in the visual field. A mere building in the foreground reminds us how massive that familiar compadre out in space truly is. Higher up, left to float above in lonesome isolation, its presence is felt, but its impact is blunted.

Sometimes loving seems like no big deal, but bring some of that perspective into the picture and we can't help but notice, and be reminded. It can be a moment of joy, a gesture, a touch, the deepest expression of passion, or the everyday proximity of sharing busy lives taken for granted until you find each other and embrace anew; or it can test the endurance of your love with failings, with tragedy, with the whims of circumstance and fate conspiring to keep you apart. Still, when someone is a part of you, no distance is too great for *your* constant moon to say: I know this journey is hard, but keep watching out the window; I'm following along, making every turn, keeping an eye out, sharing the ups and downs.

As we hurtle through life, sometimes that special person is out of sight, below the horizon, but we know he or she will always come back. Sometimes our loved one is shining bright, or maybe we see only a sliver while slanted light and skewed perception play tricks with our eyes. Sometimes, even, in the new moon, we see only darkness, and we have to strain to find what we know in our hearts is still there.

You see, even when the moon is black, or halfway around the world, we know it, too, is always there. We can feel it bending us to our core and shifting our oceans with massive tides.

So pause for a moment, consider this simple truth, then say thanks to your very own constant moon.

And remember: no matter how far, that ol' moon is always close enough to reach out and touch.

That ought to make you jump for joy.

Still, I think that moon-jumping cow must have been a real lunatic.

ROOM FOR CHARLIE

An Essay by
Stephen Geez
StephenGeez.com
Art by D.R. Wagner

I'll bet old Charlie reminds you of someone you know. A friend of my parents', he was an odd bird, a good-natured feller with a long neck and a red splotch around his mouth. He waddled more than walked and, though no dancer, he did like to wiggle his tail.

Charlie was a wild white goose.

My parents first spotted him standing vigil in the tall grass of Guntersville Lake, watching over his dead companion who had washed ashore. Geese mate for life, so Charlie wouldn't leave her, following sadly as my father carried her remains into the woods and buried her. After a while, the lonesome bird returned and continued his vigil, mourning in a way we may never fully understand.

Charlie lost his will to fly after that, never again spreading his wings to reach for the sky. Maybe it reminded him of what he'd lost, soaring in the heavens with his partner, living the good goose life, the clouds no place for inconsolable grief.

One day my parents barbecued with friends, and Charlie finally moved, waddling over to claim a seat on the lawn. Their little dog sniffed and yipped, but Charlie kept a wary eye on the hairy nuisance until both decided they might just get along. Charlie gratefully ate whatever people tossed him, eventually following the kids around as they played, honking his approval, thrilled for a chance to join in the fun.

Charlie became a regular fixture, sleeping near a boathouse and tagging along, like some dignitary's Secret Service escort, whenever Mom walked the dog. He'd chase a ball, swim out to watch my father fish, even try to help mow the lawn or paint a shed or filet some crappie, offering encouragement and advice, if not useful assistance. He'd chase squirrels from the bird feeder and coots off the lawn, and he liked to relax on the pier at sunset to watch barges float off into the night.

Whenever the Canada geese passed through, Charlie would honk up a gracious welcome, swimming out to catch up on the goose news and swap goose tales with his buddies. They mostly ignored him, though, this gander without a mate, the odd man out, a fifth wheel, leftover sock with no match. He'd watch sadly when they moved on, returning to his spot and waiting for the next dog-walking, watching down the road for weekenders who might bring grandkids ready to play.

For years Charlie stayed at the cove, offering his companionship, patiently hoping for attention, unaware of trivialities like plats and invisible property lines. He spent most his time sitting by the tall grass, his eyes closed, that long neck stretched high, his gentle face turned up toward the warm light . . . those moments when he found his own place in the sun.

Charlie slowed down as he got older, watching the kids more than joining in their play, sometimes skipping the dog-walk to sit quietly in his spot. Toward the end, he disappeared into the woods several times, maybe to be alone, maybe because he understood something many of us would never expect from a simple goose.

The day Charlie didn't return, my father found him with his head laid gently on his mate's grave. I hope he spent his last moments imagining again how it felt to soar into the clouds, wing-to-wing with his life's companion.

Charlie and his mate are buried together now, there by the lake where geese pause in their seasonal migrations, where weekenders still bring grandkids to enjoy life by the water.

Another big white goose showed up last year, acting like he intends to stay. Nobody knows his story, but they call him Clarke. Mom finds him outside the kitchen window every morning, that long neck stretched up to greet her with a howdy-do. He's a good old bird, too.

I'll still bet old Charlie reminds you of somebody you know, somebody who's lost his mate, the odd man out, fifth wheel, leftover sock. Spend some time with him, and you'll probably find he likes catching up on the news and swapping tales, trying not to show his sadness when it's time for you to move on.

He might be alone right now, maybe with his eyes closed, face toward the warm light, waiting patiently for attention.

Everybody has a bit of old Charlie in him . . .

We all need to find our own place in the sun.

FUNGUS AMONG US

An Essay by
Stephen Geez
StephenGeez.com
Art by Dizzy

The world's biggest critter is a shameless flasher.

I'm not talking about fauna such as the great whales, or giant flora like the magnificent sequoia. Nor am I referring to architecture along the lines of coral reefs, some of which are counted as the largest critter-built structures on Earth, under-oceanview condos for trillions of tiny polyps who've perfected the art of working together.

No, what I'm talking about is the mighty fungus, which experts about all things fungal tell us grows bigger than any other terrestrial being we'll ever encounter. Individual specimens have been found to extend through areas covering multiple acres. Yikes! That's *big*.

Granted, fungi aren't widely regarded as particularly smart, though as far as we know they might be keeping a low profile for reasons known only to them. I doubt any has ever lurked in some dark alley waiting to jump on someone, and I've never heard of them running in dangerous street gangs; so except for a few specialized varieties adapted to pester human skin, they generally go about their business with little fanfare.

Still, I always thought the mushroom portion of a fungus could look quite cool, especially given the myriad possible shapes and patterns. I've enjoyed eating more than a few, too, but only with assurances my choices passed non-toxic muster.

Fungi do have a propensity to move in quickly when nature needs them, and they serve an extremely useful purpose. They're masters at converting the complex structures of recently deceased organic matter into simpler ones, the better to return fundamental nutrients to the bottom of the food chain, a role without which we at the high end would have trouble finding sustainable resources to eat.

For a long time I thought those nifty little capped stalks that would shoot up in moist dark areas represented the bulk of your average mushroom, individual fungi unto themselves. It turns out that the body of your typical fungus generally lives underground, or in and through rotting logs and other compost, and that what occasionally pops up into plain sight are only the, um, naughty bits.

Yes, the parts we admire, the stools claimed by toads for casual sittin'—those tasty morsels we harvest and eat—are actually just the reproductive organs. They appear simply for the purpose of spreading the fungal seed—or spores, to be precise.

I guess what most arouses a randy fungus to raucous debauchery is plying it with water, usually of the rain variety, but any kind from designer label to everyday garden-hose will do the trick. Cheaper than wine, for sure, water's the elixir for a process that has predated controlled fermentation by many hundreds of millions of years. Dim lighting helps, too, but candles are a no-no, and last I checked, nobody had studied the effects of romantic music and whispered promises on your typical fungus.

I don't know about you, but since learning this I certainly see them differently when I spot a patch of 'shrooms thrusting themselves up from the soil.

But I also think, Wow, what a noble creature. Adapted to fill a critical niche, it has succeeded in ways that make it virtually immune to extinction. The next planetary house-cleaning cataclysm might well relegate us to the fossil record, but even then you can bet that your friendly fungi will be there to help us along.

So what do we make of that unassuming sprout we call the mushroom?

Well, in a word, soup. Or a nice wine-infused sauce. I like them sauteed, or breaded and deep-fried. Of course, dried and sliced for a salad is always a treat, and don't get me started on what they can do for a piping hot pizza.

And remember not to be fooled by the lowly mushroom's low-key demeanor. Next time you find yourself gazing upward, awestruck by the immensity of a giant redwood, look down around its trunk. You might just spot a few hints of that true leviathan lurking below.

So next time you notice a wild patch of, well, excited mushrooms flashing their naughty bits, bewilder your friends with a catcall or two:

"Get a room!"

"Hey, you! Put some clothes on!"

"What? Is *that* all you got?"

Then skedaddle quickly before some turf-protecting mushroom gang feels disrespected enough to come after you.

I hear some o' them fellers is *real* big.

DANDELION FLUX

An Essay by
Stephen Geez
StephenGeez.com
Photo by Scott Watson

Some say keep your head down.

Any situation with the potential for competition and conflict tends to divide us between those willing to "stick your neck out" and those who prefer the less-risky "keep your head down" approach.

I think of this when I look at dandelions, and I remember

something my 7th-grade science teacher said.

That was back when only the most progressive public-school educators dared to explain the more politically sensitive applications of astute observation, reasoned hypothesis, and rigorous testing. Because my teacher was fascinated by how species adapt to change, and how new strains diverge as old ones sometimes die off, he suggested we spare a few minutes every summer to observe that obstinate bloom known, when stripped of its common expletives, simply as . . . the dandelion.

Suburban dandelion sightings had been rare in the decade prior, at least in our 'hood, but the past few years had seen an explosive proliferation of these determined invaders. Suburban lawns accustomed to shrugging off nuisance incursions from the nefarious likes of mere crabgrass suddenly found themselves overrun by an onslaught of those weedly blossoms in bright yellow, a shade we Michigan alumni call "maize." In even the smallest patch of grass, thousands of one-bloom dandelion stalks would shoot up in a matter of days, generally about 6-8 inches high.

Strikingly beautiful in neutral context, they appeared as the haughty little progeny of Sol, smiling mini-suns boasting petal coronas; but to the green-carpet obsessives, they must have looked like battalions of occupying forces, foot soldiers steadfast in their conquest of foreign lands. Given the dearth of species-specific chemical and natural weapons at the time, harried lawn-tenders usually found it easiest to mow incessantly, the better to behead the enemy and thus prevent its spread of demon seed.

Of course, that whole spreading-seeds thing is pretty much the business of dandelions.

I mean, you find a good spot, squeeze out the competition, put down some roots, crank up the photosynthesizer, and lure some opportunistic pollinators, then put all your energy into creating a fragile seed-ball to be scattered by the winds—and you've pretty much succeeded at being a weed. Managing to frustrate the beejezus out of a two-legged sod-lover, well, that's just gravy. For the dandelion, though, the risky part is sticking their necks out, a blatant ploy to lap up buttery sunshine and shout a lookee-lookee yoo-hoo to brigades of buzzy bugs and bumbly bees.

Of course, that's when the lawnmowers would get them.

My teacher predicted that we twelve-year-olds could, in our lifetimes, observe some anecdotal evidence of species adaptation by watching the lowly dandelion. Where that tall, stiff stalk had once proven advantageous for rising above wild grasses, in the nutrient-rich environs of otherwise hostile lawns it would prove a fatal vulnerability. As thousands of their brethren perished, the survivors left to propagate would be those who somehow resisted the blade—or avoided it altogether. He predicted that new generations of dandelions would favor the characteristics of flexible and/or shorter stems, the latter being the preferred strategy of the keep-your-head-down crowd.

I don't know what turf experts have documented over the decades, but my own informal observations of very limited samples do give the impression that both strategies have proved successful. I see lawns studded with maize flowers hunkering at sod level, and the few blooms who stick their necks out let the mower simply knock them down until danger passes and the sun coaxes them back to the upright position.

We study how domestication has turned early versions of nutritional plants into what we know today as the corns and tomatoes and beans and other comestibles found in supermarket bins, and we adapt our herbicidal and other eradication strategies to target only those nuisances we hope to avoid. Sure, we understand the whole process in this ongoing weed/man territorial joust, but dandelion prevention still requires constant dogged vigilance, and even then there'll thrive a patch of those Machiavellian little yellow-clad invaders watching and waiting nearby, biding their time.

You have to give them credit, and maybe even think about the secrets to their success.

In situations such as the workplace, sticking one's neck out can prove effective, a way to attract positive attention, but it can also make us a target. Smart buds among us consider long-term goals, weigh the risks and benefits, and decide when it might prove wiser to keep it on the down-low while biding time for that chance to shoot a move.

I guess the best school teachers make similar choices every day, too. I recall that mine was told to cool it on the species-adaptation talk, to keep his head down for a while. The times are changing, and with so many religious leaders now acknowledging that faith doesn't necessarily conflict with what science can teach us, those skirmishes about what real teachers dare teach thankfully grow ever more isolated. I suspect we'll always live in a world where the loudest opinions tend to come from those who never make any serious effort to observe, to learn, and to understand.

Or from those who never met the right teacher.

Mine accomplished his goal, and now many of us, his legion of students, see things we might never otherwise notice.

So when I see those lawn-taunting happy-face dandelions on sunny summer days, I applaud my 7th-grade science teacher, and thank him for sticking his neck out.

HATTER-MAD

An Essay by
Stephen Geez
StephenGeez.com
Art by Dizzy

It's been said that the idiom "mad as a hatter" harkens back to the days when haberdashers used mercury in the processing and assembly of their pate-topping creations, and that prolonged exposure tended to make many hatters act somewhat—if not outright—*non compos mentis*.

I recall my public-school science teachers (let's just say back when bellbottoms and hippie hair were popular) giving us vials of pure mercury to use in experiments. We inquisitive students certainly enjoyed playing with the stuff, liquid metal cold to the touch, psychedelic fun on any flat surface. It never occurred to us—nor apparently to school officials—that certain protective measures might be in order when handling so toxic a substance. Verbal cautions—"Don't swallow any, and wash your hands"—I think, were considered sufficiently prudent.

I enjoyed a relatively safe childhood, owing a lot to parents who, like most, tried to anticipate life's hazards and protect me from them, their efforts including numerous verbal cautions of the "Don't run with scissors" variety. I used to divide my free time between reading books and prowling the wilderness to search for all manner of varmints in their still-natural, pockets-amid-suburbia habitats, both kinds of activities being reasonably considered non-toxic.

Some adults couldn't make the same claim in those days, much to our national shame. Way too many workers were exposed to chemical hazards fitting the categories of didn't-know, should-have-known, knew-but-didn't-worry, and (worst of all) knew-but-kept-it-secret.

At least I *thought* I was safe.

My favorite critter-crawly hangout sprawled behind our newly minted city hall, a pocket-amid-suburbia parcel of dense woods, clear streams, wildflowered clearings, and several shallow ponds. I knew the place and its cycles well: the exact stumps where snakes produced writhing wads of little slitherers, glassy shallows serving tadpoles an all-day skeeter-catered larvae buffet, grassy stretches hosting fat toads and sleek leopard frogs gathering so thick that any intrusion would set off a hopping frenzy, sandy washes inviting turtles to jostle for space in the sun, and sweeping branches nestling all manner of colorful birds and their cheeping chicks.

Decades later, that area suffered a thorough bulldozing for the installation of a park, complete with the requisite macro-mosaic of baseball diamonds. I'm not sure that constitutes site improvement, but it did serve a growing constituency demanding such facilities near to home.

Problem is, after numerous years of operation, soil on the ballfields was discovered to be toxic, contaminated with several substances, including dangerous concentrations of arsenic, lead, and mercury. Only then did a local old-timer come forward with photos from way back showing hundreds of rusting chemical drums and other caustic debris dumped on that plot by, of all people, our infrastructure stewards at the county road commission. Now local children are being medically tested, and the park has been closed indefinitely. Fences and other formidable barriers protect local citizens from walking through what used to be their own neighborhood open-space oasis.

And I can't help but remember all those days being the only soul out there digging for critter grub and wading through crayfish ponds just a few short summers after massive amounts of toxins were allowed to seep into the same soil and groundwater. Worse, many years later I did experience a chronic medical problem that could reasonably be explained by childhood exposure, though I doubt I'll ever know for sure.

It seems our quest to build a quality community often gets a bit ahead of itself, not only destroying much of what should have been preserved, but literally planting the germs of danger that lurk in wait for future generations to discover the hard way, sometimes too late.

We've made some progress, yet now children are scavenging

recoverable elements from our toxic high-tech trash exported to Africa and Asia—as if that's sending it far enough away. We continue to lace our lands and waters and skies with the toxins that infiltrate nature's cycles, many to settle eventually in our oceans, the nurseries of our life and ultimate source of our sustenance. We allocate funds for clean-up, but not nearly enough, and too often allow those charged with this important mission to falter in their responsibilities.

Most of the time, we don't notice what's going wrong, except when we reach the tipping point, those occasions when something draws our attention: food supplies tainted by mercury, massive stretches of coral reef dying off, asbestos fibers drifting through old-building air, lead in the paint of foreign-manufactured toys . . .

And poisonous ball diamonds threatening youngsters just steps from their own homes.

That guy with pictures of the old road-commission dumpsite assumed "they" had cleaned it up before installing a park where his children's children might watch a toad hopping into tall grass, or a butterfly flitting from clover bloom to bloom.

He was wrong.

And that leaves me wondering: How much can any of us afford to keep assuming?

COTTON DANDY

An Essay by
Stephen Geez
StephenGeez.com
Art by Dizzy

Few people remember the first time they explored the confectionary wonder in a giant wad of cotton candy. Most of us were too young, and certainly not sufficiently sophisticated to understand the deception behind so much taste-tickling fun. Watch any young first-timer, though, and you can see all the stages of true discovery.

First come the big eyes, sheer awe at the unbounded promise of a massive treat bigger than one's belly.

Then flaring nostrils, as swirling aromas hint of sweet cherries, electric blueberries, or the tartest of tropical limes.

Then arching brows, a conundrum of missing mass, candy so light it barely resists floating away on summer breezes.

Next comes the lookaround, a confirming search for cues: Are others really eating this stuff? How does a body fit so big a prize into one's suddenly undersized taster?

Finally we see radiant delight, the realization that it tastes quite good, indeed; that it feels good, too; and that it goes down smooth and sweet . . . and surprise! there's room enough for more!

Cotton candy represents the art of faking real, spinning and spinning the inconsequential into an image boasting of substance, yet consisting almost entirely of air.

I think of cotton candy when I watch a political rally. Don't get me wrong; I believe some of our most successful politicians stand among our greatest of citizens: brilliant leaders with vision, true believers in their own ability to help us achieve our collective goals.

Still, among those greats, the *good* politicians are also cotton *dandies*. These are the ones who understand that elections are more about, well, style than substance; about presenting what tastes good and pretending it's real; about who can spin the biggest, prettiest promises, even if they're mostly air and always leave room for more.

I mean, you don't see youngsters lining up at a carnival booth clamoring for boiled tripe or spinach on a stick.

Ask any politician a question, and in the campaigner's mind

it'll be categorized to match the closest flavor, a pre-packaged position statement already focus-grouped and rehearsed. It's like software analyzing and classifying a query—subject: orange—then hardware dripping the proper color into a spinner, resulting in the most impressive confection of concern topped by sugary hope and reassuring promises of better and more.

And just to make sure it all goes down smoothly, aides are standing by in the spin room to help spin you some more.

Truly, I don't begrudge a candidate the artful practice of twirling cotton candy. That's one of the basic requirements in passing the skills test: demonstrable expertise in diplomacy and tact, trading for advantage while giving up little more than air, then serving up a solution that provokes the big eyes of unbounded promise.

Still, too much cotton candy can make you sick. When I consider a candidate, I'm looking for recipes that make even the less-popular but more-substantial dishes at least palatable.

Candy is sweet, but when a cotton dandy starts spinning and spinning you, be careful you don't get so dizzy you forget . . .

We still live in a boiled-tripe and spinach-on-a-stick world.

TOO STUPID TO LIVE

An Essay by
Stephen Geez
StephenGeez.com
Image by Geez

Have you ever read or watched a story peopled by characters who are what I call "too stupid to live"?

I've never quite understood the attraction of these kinds of tales. The audience is supposed to invest emotional currency in rooting for total boobs who persist in displaying the savvy and finesse of a night-time moth flinging itself at a bare light bulb.

I'll bet you have seen countless examples of characters in jeopardy who apparently succeed in vanquishing their mortal threat—be it the dangerous human or killer beast—only to expose themselves without having ascertained that the antagonist truly has been neutralized. I want to shout, "Make sure it's really dead!" Do smart victims leave an unconscious kidnapper slumped against the wall *weapon in hand?* Did anyone *see* the chainsaw mangler get blown up, or is *assuming* good enough? Might that dead alien regenerate?—or spew out a legion of killer baby aliens?

Consider the risk of imperfect containment. Sure, you've handcuffed the crazed slasher to a radiator; now stop and pose for pictures, sign a few autographs—no way can the bracket holding that pipe be pulled loose. Hooray!—the big gate is closed, the behemoth and his minions locked out, plenty of time to argue about who deserves what credit before the invaders find a way over the wall. Thugs are locked in the back seat of the cop car; nobody in the history of cop cars has ever escaped by kicking out a window.

I find it hard to ride with this ilk. Sure, I understandably worry about a person with limited capacity, especially a naïve child who is scared and unprepared—but adults others depend on? I want to root for someone whose cleverness I admire, characters who contrive solutions that impress me and even catch me by surprise. I quickly grow frustrated hitching my empathy wagon to goofballs who insist on driving it off a cliff. These people are just too stupid to live.

And how do you feel about screamers? Isn't the instinctive choice generally *fight or flight?* Do real people in the real world scream hysterically like that? Sure, a slight percentage of people might, but when you're huddled with a small group whose lives depend on not being detected by the big hairy head-chomper, do you really want to trust your fate to someone whose strategy is to make a lot of noise? That strikes me as blatantly counter-intuitive. I'm more likely to support the bold soul who figures the screamer is a goner anyway, and thus opts to offer her head to the chomper so everyone else has a fighting chance. At least it would shut her up.

In reality, people vary considerably in the degree to which they maintain their composure in dangerous situations, but I like to think most can remain at least rational enough to weigh options and formulate a course of action. Hysteria is one ugly outfit to wear at a mayhem party.

I understand that sometimes stories are crafted to be campy, maybe even spoofy, but in most cases it's just bad writing to have such weak, uncreative plots that one must rely on lame characters acting stupid to create tension and peril. When the sheriff manages to kill two giant crocodiles that have lunged from the lake, only a poorly drawn character would celebrate by jumping up and down on the shore, back to the water. When antagonists with weapons are outside the cabin, hidden in the woods, don't reasonable people stay away from exposed windows? Turn off the lights?

One of my favorite hate-hims is the "leader" who insists on rushing into a dangerous situation without assessing potential harms—or formulating a Plan B, or even establishing a way to retreat. Betting it all on one risky move makes a thrilling plot only when the audience sees no other option.

Often you can spot an extra character who is there for the purpose of dumbly jeopardizing everyone else. The smart types have all but succeeded in saving everybody's lives—until it turns out the one total idiot who was warned otherwise still manages to betray the group by secretly calling someone, or telling the wrong person a secret plan, or trying to retrieve inconsequential posses-sions, or acting so foolish as to turn on a light or let a cellphone ring. Often it's the same knucklehead who squanders critical sup-plies, wastes ammo, forgets to bring the needed device, or burns the map because he or she got cold.

Another too-common, way-too-easy-to-spot role is exempli-fied by the guy on *Star Trek* wearing the red shirt. Not a regular character, easily expendable, he's there to get killed. That's sup-posed to ramp up the drama, raise the stakes for characters we care about the most, and evoke waves of anguish and sympathy from the audience. I just feel insulted. The writer(s) are overesti-mating my naïveté and failing to manipulate my emotions. At least this kind of victim usually has a decent chance of looking like a hero, especially if he or she perished without fault. Still, if I can see it coming, it's difficult to empathize with anyone who never picks up a clue. I'd rather pull for the ensign brave enough to say, "Um, you want *me* to wear the red shirt? You know, I think I'm gonna sit this one out."

If the writer establishes a dominant role for someone who has knowledge and wits, plus a natural ability to lead, it's rather cliché to saddle him or her with the archetypal naysayer. "Don't follow him! We must wait here for rescuers to come save us!" Yeah, call central casting and order a stock character from their that'll-never-work, don't-go-that-way, don't-listen-to-the-leader crew.

Most rational people entering dangerous situations avoid teaming up with people who don't see obvious signs. If anybody with common sense could spot all the clues that maybe these peo-ple are *vampires*, why feel bad for the rube who naïvely accepts an invite to their midnight party?

Then when somebody does fail to survive, where do reasona-ble characters strike a balance between mourning now and wait-ing to mourn after escaping the same fate? "I'm sorry, dear, but he's clearly dead, and you really do need to leave his body and come with us because the fire / zombies / chainsaw killer / swarm of poisonous wasps / deadly virus / mobster hit-men / searing lava / assassin robots / pack of rabid raccoons is racing this direction."

I put a lot of time and effort into creating characters for my books. I try to make them feel real. I want readers—even those who are very different and unfamiliar with the worlds my characters inhabit—to identify with enough about them to want them to succeed. We need to feel their frustrations and fears in order to share their triumphs and joys. I find it difficult to identify with another story-teller's characters when they inevitably get eaten for insisting, "Oh, it won't bite."

If I were placed in serious jeopardy, I'd like to think I would look out for others and make my best effort at saving myself. If nobody in a story can rise to that level, then I might as well pull for the giant crocodile. I mean, he does bite, and he needs to eat, too.

That ol' croc might as well eat the characters who are too stupid to live.

ONE GOOD CAR

An Essay by
Stephen Geez
StephenGeez.com
Art by Dizzy

I asked Cousin Tom if he'd like to have his old car again after all these years, a throwback to his days as a young man when he drove a (now) classic Pontiac GTO.

He nodded, then looked wistfully into the distance and re-marked, "They say in your lifetime you'll have one good woman, one good dog, and one good car. I've had the dog and the car."

Without elaborating on why he omitted one from the list, I'll just say I do remember the good dog, and that car is something I certainly would like to have owned.

Cars evoke myriad associations, not only for their drivers, but for onlookers, as well. I noticed this when I had run home to retrieve a wayward permission slip just as my scout troop pre-pared to leave school grounds for a camping trip. Luckily, Tom was nearby, so we jumped into his GTO, laid a patch of rubber, and roared off toward the parking lot, arriving before we'd even left my house. Dozens of boys rushed over to *Oooh* and *Ahhh*, ad-miring that sparkling green muscle-beast in all its powerful, growl-ing glory. Tom scored serious points on the coolness scale that day.

Clever automotive marketers have long known that most men see cars as extensions of themselves, badges of success, skins of style, powerhouses of drive, wads of cash in shiny money clips . . . and they groom them, meticulously neat or down and dirty, ele-gantly spare or festooned with strut-worthy plumage.

Women wear their cars, too, but of course the image they de-sire varies in most cases from your typical man's. Dodge tried chasing female buyers in the '50s with branded she-models, cars as fashion accessories, including handbags to match upholstery and a makeup mirror for that modern lady who wants it all. Clumsy, yes, and borderline insulting—an unintended parody that failed to score—it nevertheless led to a very sophisticated and highly specialized era of automotive targeting. Man or woman, young or old, the car companies and their promotional arms know not only how you intend to use any kind of vehicle, but how it makes you look, and how that makes you feel.

So Tom's "one good car" was that GTO from way back, and

if you ask people who have achieved a measure of success that affords them ample choices for their motoring and parking pleasure, I believe most will name a model from their younger days. I know a guy driving a Cadillac CTS-V as his spare *pleasure car*—a dream vehicle I dare say would have a shot at elevating *my* lifestyle—but he talks about his teen-years Nova with a fondness usually reserved for, well, women and dogs.

My friend Roger made his fortune, then spent years searching for the exact year, make, and model of Cutlass Supreme he'd bought as a young fellow who saved his wages for years. Finding one, he wound up spending more than he had on his first house to have that car restored and customized beyond its original perfection, indeed until it became the car he'd *imagined* while driving it all those years ago.

I think that's the secret.

We probably drove Mom's car a bit, then settled for a hooptie that might or might not have gotten us from here to there; but eventually, sometimes sooner, maybe a bit later, we managed to claim ownership of a car or truck that we *wanted*, that made us feel good behind the wheel, that made us proud to pull up in front of our friends and neighbors. We might have driven a hundred successively greater vehicles in the years since, but no other will ever be that first, and none will ever make us feel that way again.

You should have seen Roger showing me that restored Cutlass. I admit it was a beautiful thing, but half an hour into the excruciatingly detailed presentation I understood why I wasn't nearly as enthralled as he. I started having more fun when I realized what was really happening: He wasn't showing me his car . . .

He was showing me himself.

He was offering me an intimate glimpse of who he used to be, a full-circle embodiment of who he'd become.

I'd like to see Tom pull up someday in a fully restored, sparkling green, growling beast of a GTO, but even if that never happens, I won't forget how utterly cool he looked to my eleven-year-old eyes when he zoomed me into that parking lot.

If you have one good woman—or man, as it were—then that's great. I hope you have one good dog—or cat or goldfish or whatever wags a tail for you, too. Grab whoever you got and jump into your classic car for your own trip back in time.

And if *that* car's a bit out of your reach, just close your eyes and remember . . .

You know how it felt.

See? You're *still* in the driver's seat.

CULIN-ARTISTRY

An Essay by
Stephen Geez
StephenGeez.com
Art by Dizzy

We have entered the age of fully interactive media, and it sure tastes good.

Now more than ever, pleasureful stimulation of the senses provides its audience opportunities to participate, select venue, arrange elements, control pace, combine or separate pieces, choose climax and finale, and determine outcome. Of course, one medium has already been offering near-perfect interactivity for thousands of years:

The culinary arts.

Food preparation truly is an art form, one that elevates the satisfaction of a most basic human necessity, a drive stimulated internally by hunger, or externally through any of the senses: the chilly tickle of ice cream on a hot day, the staccato of sizzling bacon bringing rhythm to a dreary morn, the vision of a gourmet spread in enticing splendor, the aroma—ah, the many aromas—of vanilla bean and cinnamon, warm bread cooling on the hearth, roast beef simmering in deep broth, smoky trout fillets grilling over mesquite embers, citrus slices summoning tropical orchards to wintry climes, creamed corn bubble-blurping in an earthen crock, and the youthful exuberance in whiffs of fresh-baked pies and cakes and tortes . . .

Any symphony to stimulate the palette requires a maestro, either performing the scored recipe of another composer, presenting one of his own favorite opuses, or improvising like the spontaneous session players of free jazz.

The art of pleasing the tongue is a noble human endeavor. The community of man has devoted considerable effort throughout history to discovering more and more ingredients, ensuring ample supply year-round, maintaining maximum quality, and inventing new ways to serve. Nearly every home devotes an entire room to preparing food, plus another to consuming it, a process that is certainly ritualized and often communal, with each participant controlling his own sensory immersion.

All people pick up the rudiments of food preparation, then start a lifelong process of learning from others, developing their own techniques and identifying their own preferences. Taking the best from those who have "cooked" before, each develops an individual talent that belongs exclusively to one. For some, their skills remain rudimentary. Others raise it to high art, which often sparks a desire to share with others.

At the top, we find the master chef, a trained and practiced soul who has transcended mere skill to stretch his creativity, a performer for the famished masses, every presentation a masterpiece appealing to all the senses, an exquisite homage to taste.

My friend Kent Casey is one.

He revels in the interactivity of culinary expression.

He appreciates a medium where people start with a menu, choose the courses, then customize further—from dressing flavors to entree cooking times to dessert toppings. Once served, they add their own spices, decide how much and how fast to eat, then fully interact with their meal, taking a bite of this or a nibble of that, maybe pushing aside those while devouring all of these and saving some of the rest for last. What and when and how much they drink adds liquid syncopation to their selections. Chefs at Kent's level maximize the choices and ensure an elegant experience where each diner ultimately takes charge.

Top chefs performing for larger audiences earn their own venues, restaurants or clubs where they develop signature dishes, evolving menus that shift over time in response to customers' raves, operations as elaborate as the tour production of a musical group. A full support staff helps pull together all the elements needed for a grand performance that embodies the artist's vision and pleases the crowds.

Kent has done that and more, working his way up from supporting "back-up" roles, sometimes with famous chefs boasting well-known names, then succeeding as the executive chef designing his own menu for a new restaurant. Each proved a grueling, time-consuming commitment, so when family obligations urged him toward a lighter schedule, I was proud to see him take his art to people who deserve a measure of culinary pleasure often missing from their day-to-day living: the residents of retirement homes and assisted-living communities, an audience quite easy for him to find in the greater Tampa area.

Accepting the challenge at several facilities, he transformed their dining operations by listening to their preferences, accommodating their special needs, and finally dazzling them with gustatory delights. Where unhappy residents had customarily avoided the on-site facilities' pabulum, participation soon skyrocketed, and many made Kent's dining rooms into regular destinations, even treating their family and friends, a way for loved ones to share the kind of joy only tasty food can uniquely offer.

In my own coming dotage, I should be so lucky.

Now Kent relishes the selective flexibility found in also sharing his art with clients in their homes. As a "Personal Chef," he's thrilled to have finally achieved maximal interactivity. Just as you might cook for your own family and friends, expressing your own creativity to show you care, he gets to visit people's homes and perform for small audiences, each occasion a unique opportunity to listen to their wants, then amaze them with his concepts, sticking around only long enough to drink hearty drafts of their afterglow. From romantic dinners to grand celebrations, he plays a role central to the very best of the human condition.

Of course, a little something to, you know, help pay the bills is important, too, but that just affords him more chances to make new friends, discover new tastes, try new ideas, and orchestrate tasting events to raise awareness and funds for his favorite causes, such as breast-cancer research.

Culinary arts is literally the medium for which people hunger, and while a pleasing presentation can bring deep satisfaction, the desire inevitably returns. It's the fundamental cycle of survival, claiming its place in the base of any hierarchy of needs, yet aspiring to the pinnacle of self-actualization. It's a means to survival lifted to an exultation of esthetics.

Wonderfully prepared foods touch all aspects of our lives. Every taste evokes impressions: melodies, images, fleeting nuances, associations, memories, even people near and far, past and present. Hunger makes us anticipate, just as each course satisfies one moment while teasing us with the next. A great meal takes us to our own place, dances us to a theme, elevates, varies, infuses, and always questions . . . then reaches a crescendo and floats us through the coda of dessert.

I've attended incredible concerts, viewed great art, watched phenomenal films, read the most moving books . . .

And savored the singular pleasure of having my friend cook for me.

And still, in the truest form of interactive media, I accepted the gift of *his* art . . . and made it my own.

Gosh, how lucky for me that I have such good taste.

TEACHERS MEME WELL

An Essay by
Stephen Geez
StephenGeez.com
Art by Dizzy

Everybody teaches, everybody learns.

It's what we do. We discover, investigate, understand, and pass along our memes so each generation can benefit from and build upon the collective knowledge.

"Meme" is a concept that first intrigued me in anthropology courses at university in the mid-1970s. Usually credited to gene-aficionado Richard Dawkins, the term derives from the Greek for "to imitate." In studying how species increase their chances of physical survival by passing along the most adaptive of genes, he noted how humans also enhance our ability to thrive culturally by passing along the most effective of our memes—and our collective knowledge, complex ideas that serve purposes so useful that they endure through our desire to pass them along.

Our genes have found advantage in giving us the longest of childhoods, an extended period of parental and communal support allowing time enough to learn. While we begin by observing, absorbing, testing, then responding to and manipulating the environment, we simultaneously discover, practice, and master the memes governing our tribe's means of communicating with one another, culminating in language—the entree to literature, science, and the arts. In many ways, language is our greatest achievement, our means to achieve a complexity of interaction and understanding far exceeding "Don't eat the red berries" and "Hey, hot stuff, wanna get jiggy?"

As we cultivate language skills, our capacity to learn blossoms exponentially. The combination of language and experience is how we learn what others would teach, knowledge gleaned from our families, members of the community, our everyday peers, and of course those individuals we call "teacher."

The very concept of teacher is a remarkable meme, a role clearly defined, designated, devoted, compensated, and allocated time and resources to operate in a structured environment. We appreciate the laudable goals of teachers: pass along our collective knowledge; spot, spark, and nurture each individual's quest for understanding; govern social development to discourage harmful behaviors and promote personal growth; and foster a desire both to learn and to share what we know with others. I agree with the legions who consider this job to be arguably the most important in our society. Just look at what we've accomplished with our memes, which is possible only if those very memes include what we know of learning, and what we've learned about teaching.

Our educational prowess has advanced us far beyond the days of mere rote memorization. We've recognized the value in participatory learning, helping students discover for themselves, providing direct access for seeing the hows and understanding the whys. We have witnessed the dangers in believing everything we're told, so we teach critical thinking, the ability to evaluate information and its sources to fashion understanding and perspectives that are most relevant. We search for the memes that mean the most to each of us, the memes worth preserving through others.

Great teachers introduce us to possibilities, open new portals to worlds barely imagined, then fan smoldering questions and fuel new interests. They help us discover that *we* are in charge of our own learning, and they help us develop the habit of always seeking greater understanding.

Great teachers distill umpteen hours of their own learning into the few hours of instruction that most benefit their students, which allows time for each new generation to advance beyond the collective wisdom of their own teachers.

Some teachers earn paychecks and enjoy formal titles; others simply move among us, unrecognized, often unappreciated, yet always available.

As much as the greatest teachers find in us that which we hunger to know, the best students find in teachers that which they hunger to share.

I will always be grateful for my teachers, even those I've yet to find; and I try my best to pay forward their efforts, teaching others when I recognize that hunger for the knowledge and skills I humbly believe I might offer.

We should all take a moment every now and then to express our appreciation for those who deemed us worthy of their earnest efforts to play even the smallest part in helping each of us progress toward our limitless potential.

And be grateful for the best ones. They're still teaching us, even after they're long gone.

How is that possible? you wonder. Here's a meme you can pass along:

The greatest teachers teach us how to learn.

GRAFFITUM

An Essay by
Stephen Geez
StephenGeez.com
Art by Dizzy

Scurrying between obligations and opportunities as a newly minted University of Michigan undergraduate way back in the day, I noticed a puzzling depiction painted on an Ann Arbor side-walk. Three-odd decades later, I find myself pondering it again, recalling that brief flash of trifling curiosity amid weightier thoughts and grander mysteries.

Or maybe I'm just taking a moment now to see things differently.

The graffitum appeared to be a pair of cartoonish eyes amid several curved slashes, obviously a work in progress, or maybe—given the illicit nature of such artistic expression—simply a case of *imago interruptus.* Dozens of spottings later, I did stop for a moment to consider it, even to look about for clues. A typical iron fence lined one side of the walk, a row of money-grubbing double-headed parking meters the other, beyond which stretched an unremarkable street and parking garage. Move along, nothing to see here.

We tend to zoom through life awash in streaming messages, ideas and images hurled our way by people who want us to hear, to see, to think, to understand what they know; yet I find that often what intrigues me most is the forlorn concept left not fully stated, the unfinished draft of a notion never expressed. On any of those occasions, someone did succeed in getting my attention, but the overriding confluence of circumstance and fate somehow intervened to leave me wondering and, too often, frustrated and disappointed. Had I been fully informed, I might well have dismissed the communication, but not given the chance, I'll never know.

In the early '90s I taught a prison Story Writing class. There among the wrongly convicted, the mis-convicted, and the guilty as sin—but mostly repentant—I discovered that small segment who not only felt they had something insightful and important to say, but who also proved eager for help learning interesting and effective ways to say it.

Understanding they faced considerably more formidable

obstacles than most of their attention-seeking competitors, I cautioned them that the U.S. Supreme Court's affirmation that even incarcerants retain their 1st Amendment rights of self-expression means only that they're guaranteed an opportunity to write and submit, but that no Constitution guarantees them an audience. Given the requirements of outside support and generally elusive serendipity, two additional elements would be needed for their potential success: having something meaningful to say—or at least entertaining, if not both—and a presentation forged with skill and considerable effort.

I know that even after years of flinging my own words, I still expend more energy and incur more expense chasing new audiences—and trying to maintain those I've already tenuously captured—to read my stories and books, the former given freely as enticement, the latter for sale in hopes the debtors' wolves don't chew off my other leg.

So how hard must the graffiti artist work to find his own audience? Though he does risk prosecution—an approach deemed admirable by posterity only when the message ultimately proves righteous—he purchases (or "boosts") only the paints, then co-opts the public square to serve as his canvas. Big Business pays hundreds of thousands for billboard space that can't begin to rival the potential found in a gleaming expanse of freshly painted highway-overpass girder, the side of a building, or even an oft-trod sidewalk.

I don't have much respect for tagging, a marking of territory not fundamentally much different than dogs urinating on fence posts, but I do admire the artistry in conceptual statements, depictions of the human condition, the only opportunity a soul yearning for expression can find to say, *This is who I am, and this is what I think.* I can especially admire when the sprayed-on graphic art is borne of the belief that *We live where you built that, so its function is yours, but the veneer must reflect us.*

A central theme in several of my books explores the human need for creative expression, for finding a voice so compelling that others might listen or look. In *What Sara Saw* a wonderful young woman hurt too many ways devotes herself to understanding the nature of that power an artist infuses in his work to move others toward recognition, to provoke laughter or tears. In *Fantasy Patch* ad-agency creative director Danté wrestles with his own artistry balanced against plying his talents for commerce and to sway public opinion, a futile effort that increasingly threatens to topple him and his ideals. Like many writers, I have way more to say than I'll ever have a chance to set down, yet I often surprise and amuse myself with the odd and sometimes less-consequential choices I make for topics . . .

Like maybe a pair of eyes and slashing curves painted on an Ann Arbor sidewalk three-odd decades ago.

I did solve that mystery several years later, and while I'm sure whoever painted that image has since gone on to greater means of expression and, I hope, a rewarding measure of success, I do appreciate what he was trying to say to me.

You see, he'd noticed something, probably time and time again, and maybe he wanted simply to make sure others noticed it, too, or even to share a smile of acknowledgment with those who already had. I try to dig deep and say important things, especially in my books, but often I'm satisfied just to earn a laugh, or to point out something we might pass every day but never truly see.

I walked that same route one night after dark. A bright security light on the parking garage lit the money-grubbing double-headed parking meters, casting their shadows across the walk. Perfectly aligned, one maintained its shape and created the dark outline of . . .

Mickey Mouse.

I wonder how many times the graffiti artist noticed it before he felt compelled to bring his paints one night to fill in the eyes and mouth.

Now if I could only figure out how to encourage that anonymous pop-artist to notice my website and buy one of my books . . .

SEE WHAT NOW

An Essay by
Stephen Geez
StephenGeez.com
Art by Joe Posada

I have been experiencing an odd sort of fantasy on a fairly regular basis for most of my life. It's just a brief notion that pops up at any time, often when I least expect it. The content varies widely, depending on what kind of observation or contemplation triggers it. There is no telling who it might involve, except that it's almost surely to be someone long dead.

Now, I write stories, so I necessarily spend a goodly amount of time crafting imaginary scenarios in my mind, but this fantasy rarely rises to the level of plot. Simply put, I'm talking about envisioning how it would feel to snatch people from long ago and time-travel them forward for a brief visit to see what we have created, what we can do, how far we've come.

Often the person I'd like to guide during one of these short visits is a famous historical figure, but it could just as easily be an anonymous soul from any point in time, any place in the world. One curious aspect of this fantasy, a quirk I simply cannot explain, is that my default visitor, in the absence of picturing anyone else, is most likely to be George Washington.

Seriously. It's a shame George never got to see the many things I've imagined showing him.

I'd like to walk the USA's first president into a dark room in any modest home and tell him to figure out what that switch on the wall does. Just between us, what it does do is quite remarkable, unimaginable to people who lived just a few hundred years ago.

The obvious scenario in this kind of fantasy is to offer technology pioneers a glimpse of what their imaginations and endeavors will yield. Wouldn't it be fun to let Henry Ford or the Dodge brothers or Mr. Durant drive a Chevrolet Volt?—or hit 60 in under 3.9 in the fabulously luxurious and thrilling Cadillac CTS-V Coupe? Picture their faces gazing upon the dashboard instrumentation, then popping the hood. Take a road trip and watch them marvel, not just at the machines, but at all the infrastructure, superhighways connecting every corner of the nation, parking lots and drive-throughs and gas stations studding the landscape.

I'd like to sit with Nikola Tesla to watch a high-definition flat-screen television, then interrupt young Walt Disney's painstaking cel-animation production of "Steamboat Willie" long enough to offer him a weekend visiting IMAX theaters to see 3-D animated Disney Pixar films. I'd follow those with a screening of live-action special-effects lollapaloozas where you can't even tell what's animated and what's faked-real before sending him back to finish Willie with trembling hands.

You think Alexander Graham Bell would be impressed by cell-phone technology? Touchscreens, phone cameras with transmittable images, a phone in every pocket, calling anywhere in the world even while barreling through the desert, miles from civilization?

Sam Morse would think surely I'm pulling his leg. Invisible waves hurtling through the air? Signals bouncing off satellites floating in outer space? Huh? Now that's something to write home about.

I'd like some shots of young George Eastman marveling over digital cameras, then instant photo-printing, then testing the vast capabilities of that quirky little tool known as . . . *Photoshop*. "You think *color* stills are impressive?" I'd ask. "Check out these 4-chip video cameras. Or holograms."

Movable type was a jaw-dropper in its day, but I think Gutenberg might catch the vapors watching average Janes and Joes magically downloading books through the air to read on their Kindles. What would he think of inkjets and laser printers and photocopying and the computer-operated presses at a book- or newspaper-production plant—not to mention print-on-demand technology? Let him choose any book and watch a copy being produced while he sips a latte. Maybe show him how to surf the 'net, text and images written in *light*.

Wouldn't it be fun to travel with Marco Polo, jet-hopping around Asia for a few weeks? And speaking of jets, you think Orville and Wilbur would enjoy a few hours crossing a continent aboard the Dreamliner? Once their pounding hearts settled down, they would be ready to ride in a fighter jet, a helicopter, then watch a manned rocket launch. Oh, and if we're going to coast-to-coast the USA by air, let's save a few seats for Lewis & Clark. Window seats, thank you very much.

I could go on with the techno-tour, but I suspect by now you're thinking of some very cool examples of your own. So, what about our very survival, our health and lifespans?

I believe DaVinci would be amazed. (Still, would he find Dan Brown's books and spin-off movies a hoot?) In Leonardo's time, most considered invading the human body sacrilegious, even for intellectual inquiry to advance medical science. Would artist/inventor/anatomist DaVinci consider today's MRIs and CAT scans de rigueur, or what? Let's bring Hippocrates along and let both sit in the gallery to watch a routine hip-replacement surgery or installation of a graphite heart valve—you know, as run-ups to some *really* impressive medical interventions.

Time-forwarded kids might freak out at the notion of hypodermic needles, but their parents would rejoice over the very idea of childhood immunizations, the kind too many nowadays take for granted.

What about the arts? I have attended some phenomenal music-group concerts in my time, aural and visual extravaganzas that transport audiences to fantastic realms. I'd like to sit with Mozart at a few of these shows, introducing him to the great musicians of this age. "Yes, Amadeus, only four people are making all that exquisite sound." And what a variety of sounds they would be, pitches and tones and timbres in genres and styles unimagined in his time. "We call *that* one fusion jazz. Would you like to hear some blues?" I'd like to show Mussorgsky how his piano suite "Pictures at an Exhibition" sounds hundreds of years later, now fully orchestrated by Maurice Ravel . . . or produced all-synth by Isao Tomita, or art-rocking to the rafters as interpreted by Emerson, Lake & Palmer. I'd like to demonstrate for many of the classical composers how accessible their music has become, full orchestras held in the palm of one's hand, tuned up and ready to play anywhere, anytime.

Imagine what some of the great Renaissance artists could do with the plethora of supplies available today. Consider your average citizen engaged in an act as simple as writing on a piece of paper; quills and ink reservoirs had their day, but look at the options now, even what you might find in some 2nd-grader's backpack.

Don't some scientific greats deserve to look ahead? Charles Darwin changed how we see the world, yet he never saw the vast leaps brought by DNA sequencing and tracking. I'd settle for simply showing him how many more species we've found, and how many mysteries we've solved about the surprising ways they connect.

Copernicus and Galileo—surely they deserve a turn at the Hubble Telescope. Anyone at the forefront of our transition from flat-Earth paradigms—especially iconoclasts suffering retribution for the heretical notion of planets orbiting Sol—these people would find poetic justice in observing the size and shape and forces of the universe as we see and measure and understand it now.

And what about those who labored for millennia to sustain us? The farmer in the dell would delight at modern agriculture.

Would our ability to transform the landscape move those who lived close to nature? I'd like to scoop up a handful of natives living five-hundred years ago on an island in the big river, then put them on the observation platform of the Empire State Building. Yeah, look what we did to the place—good and bad—certainly impressive by any measure.

Countless builders have been erecting structures for many thousands of years. I'd like representatives from various periods and cultures to tour some of today's skyscrapers, then our greatest bridges, colossal river dams, the skylift up Snowbird Mountain . . . I'd like to take them down to Ground Zero to see 21st-century man's version of a phoenix rising from the ashes.

And how about manufacturing? I'm convinced progenitors of the Industrial Age deserve a tour of various modern factories, then a few days to watch select highlights from the series *How It's Made.*

You can take this fantasy other directions, too, such as coming up with reasons to bring people forward to warn them what can go wrong. Me, I prefer to keep it light. I simply appreciate how good we have it now in ways our forebears never could have fathomed.

Think about daily living in our own homes. Let's grab any culinary artist from the past and show him or her how easy it is to cook now—especially with the ubiquity of impressive appliances. Amaze your time-traveling guest with ingredients from all over the world, exotic yet accessible to the average citizen, not to mention year-round freezing and refrigerating and microwaving with modern food-supply safety measures. I'd like to take the butcher and the baker and the candlestick maker on a trip to the grocery store. "Really, people, this is just the everyday stuff. If there's anything you don't see, we have specialty shops, too."

Come on, who wouldn't be impressed by microwave popcorn?

If you invite your great-great-great-great-(twenty more greats)-grandparents to visit for a week, you better plan on explaining toilet tissue. Oh, and toilets. Me, I think they're a pretty cool aspect of living today. And don't get me started on washers and dryers and, gosh, *hot showers*, right there in pretty much every home.

Another form of my fantasy is demonstrating social progress. I'd like to show William Douglas and Susan Anthony and others how much we've moved toward equal participation for minorities and women. I'd love to arrange a meet-and-greet between some persecuted souls from the past and Ellen DeGeneres today.

Though it's always important to strive for improvements, we still ought to recognize what mankind has done about teaching our young: the system, the materials, the staffing, the value we place on supporting children and adolescents during a period of compulsory education. Youth-corrupter Socrates would spit out the hemlock, wipe his mouth, and grin like one happy teachin' Greekster.

Dewey changed the way we organize material with his famous decimal system. "Yeah, dude, it's called Google. Pick a topic and we'll see how long it takes to find a smattering of information."

Officers have been trying to solve crimes as long as criminals have been committing them. I'd like to show a few old-timey con- stables some modern forensic science.

So let's have some fun, too. The originators of the first attrac- tions at such places as Coney Island deserve to spend a few months with me zooming all the top-rated roller coasters around the world. "Yes, they go *upside down* now, and then some." Hey, let's splash down at a few water parks while we're at it. What the heck, let's explore a Universal Studios park, too, and see how we can soar beyond the real world without moving more than a few feet.

I'd like to take George scuba-diving, skydiving, ATV riding, water skiing, hot-air ballooning, bungee-jumping, mountain-bik- ing. Then we could tour every USA national park. Might as well take Teddy Roosevelt along. If you like to hunt or fish with all the latest high-tech gear, George and Teddy would appreciate the likes of depth-finders and laser scopes. It would be a hoot to make it a foursome and include someone who thousands of years ago prided himself on sharpening and throwing a man stick.

I suspect my presidential visitor would be dumbfounded by major sporting events: the venues, the crowds, the talent and skill, the zeal of the fans . . . the salaries and box office and ancillary revenue. I'm partisan, so top of my list would be an autumn afternoon joining 113,000-plus, the biggest crowd in the nation, watching the Maize-and-Blue at Michigan Stadium. Yeah, George, this is part of the college experience, rather like a life-size chess game with living pieces coached to work together in teams. We do take whimsical ideas and develop them until they are big and intense, and they make us proud.

Yet another form of my fantasy is to acknowledge the sheer accessibility of today's wonders to the average man, the raised standard of living for the working class. Even the poorest rarely want for clean water, basic sanitation, something to eat. Still, anybody who is able and willing to work expects to achieve a remarkable level of comfort compared to our ancestors'. The simplest way of living today would seem luxurious to most visitors from the past.

I would like to hit a few fast-food drive-through windows with George Washington, wowing him with such fast, accessible, and diverse treats. Would he like pizza? Nachos? Spicy chicken fingers and Buffalo wings? Hearty cheeseburgers with the works? Donuts? Ice cold Mountain Dew? I would amaze him with a surprising fact: "Your average unskilled laborer can cover the cost of this meal with less than thirty minutes' wages." Then I'd show him how affordable everyday high-quality clothing has become—silly-looking, maybe, but offering myriad choices for a few hours' pay.

On a hot August afternoon, I'd like to offer George a bowl of Swiss Chocolate Almond ice cream. I mean, what a delightfully new experience that would be. We'd try dozens of flavors, all the while sitting in a room cooled by something called air-conditioning. Oh, and you know what else would make this confection an extra-special treat? I'd have helped him deal with his serious dental problems first—at least with some modern, custom-crafted false teeth. Better yet, implants. Heck, since I'm in charge, I might as well transport him as a teenager when his real teeth can still be saved.

I would show him how to spruce up with an electric shaver, then hand him Transitions sunglasses and a credit card as we set out for a tour of D.C., including his own monument. We would talk about how the nation he helped create has since thrived, how it evolved and adapted, what works and what needs work and how, in the long run, it eventually keeps moving in the direction of liberty and opportunity.

I would tell him I wish someday hundreds of years from now someone would bring me forward for a visit, a chance to marvel—without being surprised—that so much *more* has come to pass.

Finally, I would take George Washington to a grand 4th of July celebration and remind him about Marco Polo and Chinese gunpowder and how in his time he and his brethren used this discovery in new ways to advance the cause of controlling our own destinies. As darkness washes another day from the sky, we would unfold some lawn chairs, fire up the portable grill, break open the ice chest, and settle in to watch a fabulous display featuring new ways to use gunpowder, stark symbolism evoking rockets'-red-glare images of freedom's battle reminding us that even now we continue to strive for peace.

We have a long way to go, George, but look how far we've come.

Let's paint the sky with colored fire and imagine what future generations might make of this beautiful world.

Notes To You

LIGHTHOUSE, KEEPER

An Essay by
Stephen Geez
StephenGeez.com
Photo by Scott Watson

A lighthouse is your friend.

You don't have to captain a ship to need one. In fact, given

GPS and other advancements in instrument navigation, light-houses rarely, if ever, actually guide ships in the dark. What keeps them important to us now transcends mere utility; it is conceptual, a notion of time and place, the evocation of belonging.

The USA boasts many of them, Michigan the most, Wisconsin not far behind, some in disrepair, a few at least somewhat re-stored. They're tourist destinations, photo subjects, the iconic identities of myriad shoreline communities. People love light-houses, often adopting a particular favorite, acknowledging it as an old and trusted friend.

So what is this fascination with those towers of light?—some reaching toward the sky, others stout and squat, all dependable and, dare I say, loyal.

Some aficionados offer tongue-in-cheek allusions to some variation of Freudian phallic infatuation, but I don't buy that. Sometimes that train steaming into a tunnel simply needs to reach the other side.

Lighthouses certainly are picturesque, focal points symboliz-ing man's determination to rise against the vagaries of nature, de-marcations dividing land from water, above from below.

For many they conjure romantic notions of a seafaring past, adventures sailing the mane, navigating by starlight while loved ones bide time on widows' walks watching hopefully for any af-firming sign.

Many are fascinated by the notion of a lighthouse keeper, that lonesome but determined old soul tending the flame, an eternal duty accepted by one best left to dwell alone at the fringe.

We look at a lighthouse and wonder about its stories. How many nights did this one make the critical difference? How many lives did it save?

I've always found it paradoxical that lighthouses were built to serve two opposing functions: they warned ships away even while summoning them home. Many a captain peered into the darkness for that telltale alert: Don't come too close! Watch for the rocks, the reefs, the wrecks!

Yet often they watched for that very same light as a welcoming beacon: This way! You're almost home.

No matter the reason you might need to find one, a lighthouse's purpose can be reduced to one simple truth: it tells you where you are.

Just like a friend.

This is easy to take for granted under clear skies, while navigating the calm waters of a simple life, your days bathed in the light of rising sun; but when you find yourself in the dark, lost and feeling adrift, storms raging, a true friend warns you about the rocks and the reefs and the wrecks.

A friend tells you, I am here. You are there. Close or far apart, we are always together.

Yes, Look for me, I know the way home.

Lighthouses mean a lot of things to many people, but to all they symbolize that unextinguishable beacon, the immovable pillar rising from bedrock, solid and sure, dependable, confirming.

A lighthouse is your friend, and your friend's lighthouse is you.

So keep your own light burning bright. Someone you love might need a warning.

And you might need to find the way home.

BIRTHDAY WISH

An Essay by
Stephen Geez
StephenGeez.com
Art by Dizzy

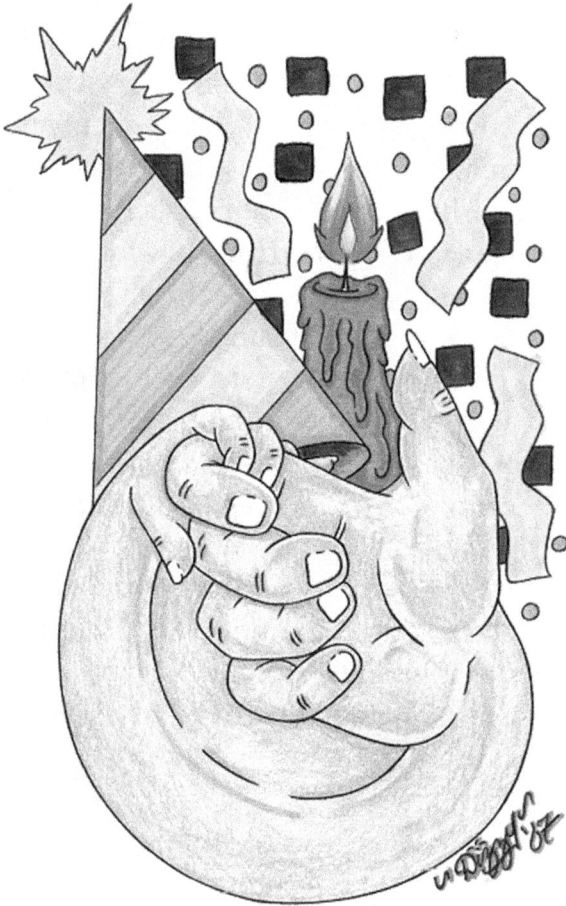

Have you ever made a birthday wish?

It's a tradition that starts very young. Children learn that each birthday is rewarding, a fine reason to celebrate, an occasion for gifts, the official opportunity to make a formal wish for even greater gain in the year to come. Eagerly anticipated, this event is recognized and acknowledged by others, an elevation of status for just that day. To a child, not much beats being "the birthday girl" or "the birthday boy."

The gift element of this rite marks milestones and conveys new "old enough for" status: the first two-wheeler, a four-legged pet, teen-rated video games, grown-up cosmetics. Aside from the largess, we also embrace this confirmation of life's milestones: reaching double-digits, becoming a teen, qualifying to join that league, passing minimum driving age, assuming the responsibilities of eighteen, flashing an ID that boasts twenty-one.

Once we have marked more than a few birthdays in our done-that columns, we inevitably notice that they seem to come at us faster. This illusion of time is explained as the comparison of fraction against the whole: to youngsters, each year represents a significant portion of all known lifetime; while to the geezer demographic, years pass as ever-shrinking increments of a marathon that now seems shorter looking back than it did to the child looking forward.

But I think this illusion also results from an increasing propensity to view time as overlapping layers. Children think of life as linear, a series of moments coming one after another, their anticipation focused solely on the what's-next: next holiday, next school-start, next school-out, next vacation . . .

Next birthday.

Maturity brings a view toward long-term multi-tiered planning, a fitting together of both complementing and competing ambitions, a balance between wants and needs—learning versus earning, seeing the world now versus starting a family and traveling later, a burst of full-time service to others versus occasional charity while advancing the self.

So there you are, assembling your own abstract jigsaw vision of life, when along comes another birthday to point out how much remains undone. The day has become a new kind of marker, a reminder to take stock, the tick of a timer powered by batteries that won't last forever. By then, most of us have lost at least one person we loved, and the abstract of ephemeral existence has become poignantly real. Sure, many expect their time to extend beyond death, and a few believe it springs from past lives before birth, but most agree that the very lifetime we cherish now on this world is finite. We will celebrate only so many birthdays, some of us more than others, none as many as we might want.

So the whole idea of a birthday wish begins to fade, relegated to the realm of childish rituals, or at least treated as an amusing diversion without the investment of honest expectation. Still, I've kept it up, and I've kept it simple. A long time ago I quit looking for "things" and started marking every birthday simply as confirmation I have lived, an occasion to hope I am lucky enough to celebrate one more next year.

So far I have a perfect record of getting my wish!

And someday that wish will have no chance of coming true.

Now I finally understand why so many eventually reject the very idea of even acknowledging their own birthdays. As those milestones come faster and faster, it's easy to forget appreciating another year, to start dreading them as ticks toward an inevitable end. Who can enjoy a leisurely stroll knowing it's to the guillotine?

There will be wrenchingly bad years, too, and who wants to "take stock" when to survive intact we've had to practice looking away from what hurts most? Maybe it's the death of a loved one, disintegration of family, setbacks to career, or even a diagnosis that promises the coming year will prove rougher, that maybe there won't be enough days left to reach another birthday.

We all want to bend time. Children age so rapidly that we wish to slow them down, to preserve those precious stages of innocence and grace, even as the youngsters are trying to speed their own growing up. Angry workers race toward retirement like frustrated prisoners hash-marking cell walls, willing to trade large slices of tangy life for a dollop of post-retirement sweet-cream before the end. But others somehow manage a modicum of contentment, if not outright moments of joy, despite the challenges that too often ironically mar the very achievement of old age.

Still, I don't understand how people can pretend birthdays don't even exist. Even to those busy crossing off time-left rather than adding to the list of days-lived, the simple fact is that a birthday comes every year, no matter how the birthday boy or girl feels about it.

So who cares?

The answer to that question, I believe, transcends time. It plants the seed of a notion that can blossom into the most exquisite of attainable birthday wishes.

Who cares, indeed.

Pretend *you* don't care about your birthday, if you must, but I'll bet somebody else does.

Really.

If your next birthday is marked by having no one who wants to wish you the best, nobody to send you a card or stop by for a visit, not a soul to throw you an embarrassing party and sing you those copyrighted words, would you rather live like that for a hundred more years than to celebrate your final birthday with people who'll invest the capital from their own wish-bank in a confirming gesture of goodwill?

I do hope you've been enjoying the most remarkable of years, and it breaks my heart to fear that maybe this one might have been especially hard, but however it measures up when you can't help but take stock, remember this one simple truth:

We live in a beautiful world, and the only reason any of us feels the pain is because we have learned to embrace the ecstasy.

We want every year to feel good and right, but if you're truly pressed to find anything wonderful about your next birthday, just look closer and I promise you'll find it in the people who care.

It might manifest as predictably as that same old card in the mail, a phone call at the customary time, or a choreographed surprise so true to its custom that all real surprise leaked out years ago.

Or it might come when you least expect it, from someone you never suspected cares.

So don't fight the pain; don't forget the joy. And don't pretend it's not your birthday, because it is, and that's a beautiful thing.

Somebody loves you, babe.

And it just might be me.

Now that's a wish come true!

So here's a *Happy Birthday* to you.

YOU GRADUATED!

An Essay by
Stephen Geez
StephenGeez.com
Image by Geez

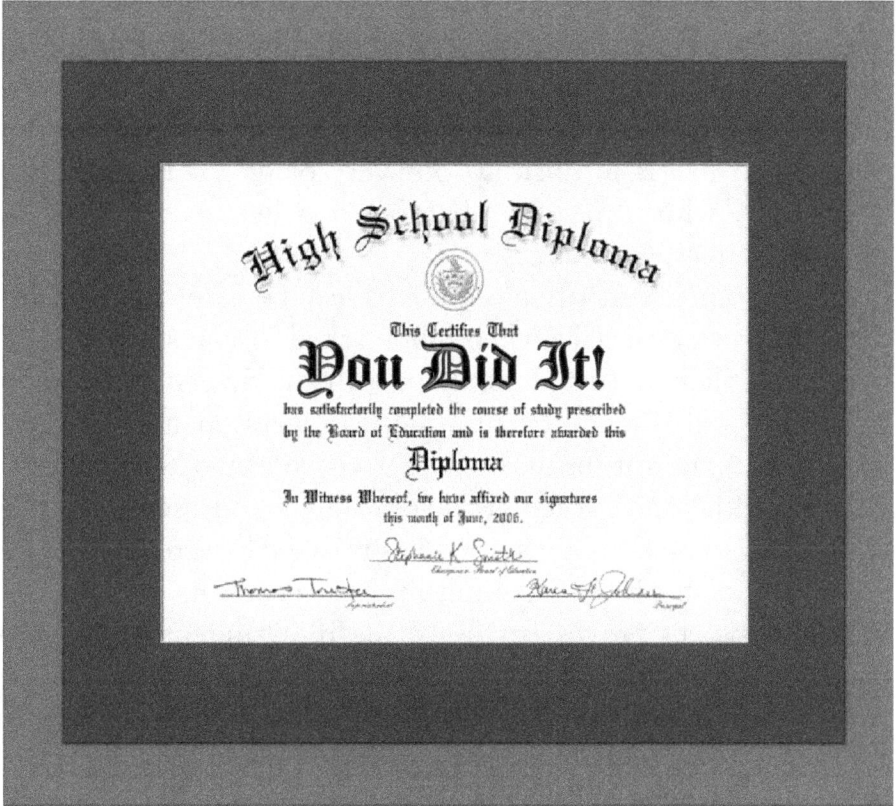

High School Diploma

This Certifies That

You Did It!

has satisfactorily completed the course of study prescribed
by the Board of Education and is therefore awarded this

Diploma

In Witness Whereof, we have affixed our signatures
this month of June, 2006.

You graduated!

You got it done.

You accepted the challenge, conformed where required,

rebelled when it served, and *never* ceded your individuality. In fact, you asserted it, taking a giant step toward knowing who you are, a lifelong process now rising to the next level. You did not simply establish your place in the world; you found new and exciting ways to make the world fit around you.

Now you understand why we wanted you to work so hard. Never in history have our societies—our cultures—placed so much emphasis on educating our citizens. Fast as we manage to cut a road, put up shelter, and tap some water, we *build a school.* We continue to expand the time and resources afforded our young to learn. We require a lot from students, offering incentives and rewarding success in ways tangible and beyond. As much as learning to live is intrinsic to our very being, so is yearning to teach those who come after, that they may live better.

And you *will* live better.

Sure, your efforts often required a leap of faith, a tremendous show of trust, especially when much asked of you seemed hardly relevant. Still, you trusted that the depth and diversity of your education would somehow matter even in ways unanticipated, not just for you, but for those you love. No way could anyone predict the breadth and reach of your life's odyssey, so even though *our* guesses might sometimes prove askew, remember that the mere fact of *your* accomplishment carries its own weight. When a subject proves frivolous, the best student nevertheless nurtures skills in the all-encompassing art of mastery, in embracing a series of increasingly challenging goals, then developing the means to achieve them. Sometimes the details of what you learn are not as important as the effort you put into becoming a learner. Graduating proves you did that. However you choose to use it, people will respect your diploma because *you earned it . . .*

Because *you* got it done.

Your education proves you are a better citizen now, a full member of the tribe sharing our common values. You are equipped with invaluable skills, able to contribute, to pass along. You have learned to develop your talents, even those not yet discovered, not yet revealed. You have tasted the exhilaration in expressing your curiosity, your creativity, your ideas. You have asked the questions and realized that answers always lead to ever greater mysteries, many of which you will spend a lifetime answering for yourself.

You didn't just get it done; you got it started.

You started something big that never stops growing bigger, so whether you continue your formal schooling or chase the challenges of exciting new directions, this moment marks an important milestone in your life. Do not consider graduation a reason to pause. Keep the momentum. All you desire, all you achieve, it all requires diligence, your determination to reach beyond what you know, what any of us know.

Your greatest skills now *are* the all-encompassing art of mastery, of embracing a series of increasingly challenging goals, then developing your own unique means to achieve them. The possibilities are limitless.

Just *imagine* what you can do.

So, congratulations, graduate. The family of man applauds you, and we who love you are prouder than words convey. You did it.

You got *that part* done.

Remembrance

FAMILY RECIPE

An Essay by
Stephen Geez
StephenGeez.com
Art by D.R. Wagner

Fruitcakes are the gift many people love to hate, but every Christmas my friend Paul's mom, Elizabeth, always cooked up what seemed like hundreds for family and friends.

Wrapping them in plastic, she tied them with red and green ribbons, a festive holiday look to mirror the twinkle in her eyes.

Fruitcakes are known to take on lives of their own, passing from one person to the next, sometimes lingering long enough to carbon-date. Cut one open, if you dare, and divine its age just as you'd count the rings of some ancient tree.

Elizabeth never pressed her lucky recipients for reports on their flavor. Maybe she sensed that at least a few appreciated them more as souvenirs, symbols of her affection, not so much mere items for callously *eating*. What mattered is that everybody in her thoughts got one, delivered with a proud smile and wrapped in love, a present from this woman who used her recipes to nourish souls as much as bodies.

The tradition was passed down by Elizabeth's mom, who had learned it from her own aunt. With nobody sure how many generations back it goes, I wouldn't be surprised to learn an early version of the recipe, scripted on papyrus and stored in an urn, has been unearthed during some distant archaeological dig.

Eventually Paul's father lost his hearing and got to where he couldn't see very well. Then Elizabeth's diabetes put her in a wheelchair and robbed her of her sight, so Paul moved back home that autumn to help care for them.

As Christmas approached, Elizabeth mentioned how much she wished she could hand out those fruitcakes again. Saddened by having to break the tradition, she reminisced about helping Grandma when she was a little girl. Tears welled in her eyes as she talked about her fruitcakes, admitting that eating them isn't what matters, that it's cooking up some love and sharing it with people who mean the most to her.

During her nap that afternoon, Paul searched through two boxes stuffed with hundreds of recipes filed in no particular order. He finally found it, flour-crusted, yellow with age, and difficult to read. He went out and bought the ingredients, then set about mixing, determined to make her a batch to give away. Paul's never been known for his culinary finesse, and most family recipes require a dollop of magic beyond what's actually written down, so he finally had to wake her, confessing his plan and asking her to help.

They spent the rest of the afternoon making fruitcakes. She took charge, while Paul served as her eyes and hands. They didn't need that old recipe card; Elizabeth knew this one by heart.

She glowed with pride as she handed them out, accepting kisses and thanks, hugging back with newfound strength despite her frail condition. She'd probably felt that way every year, but this marked the first time Paul finally seemed to understand.

Several days after Christmas, Elizabeth required hospitalization, but there was little that could be done, and she took a turn for the worse. In a stark, antiseptic room far from the familiar aromas of her kitchen, Paul lost his mother, and the world lost a friend.

Gathered at the house after the funeral, Paul and his siblings carefully copied her fruitcake recipe, all vowing to carry on the custom. Several of them did, too—for a couple of years. Busy with their own lives and still discovering their own unique ways to celebrate, they gradually let the fruitcake tradition slip away.

Some things will never leave us, though. Elizabeth's children, like everyone she touched, will always carry on with a more important tradition: living the way she taught. Devotion to our families, integrity, loyalty, and love for each other . . . these are what she passed on to the next generation. These are truly Elizabeth's recipe for life.

Everyone lucky enough to receive one of Elizabeth's fruitcakes now cherishes the memory of her face lighting up as she presented her traditional treat, wrapped in plastic and tied with red and green ribbons . . .

A family recipe, the reminder of those last precious moments my friend spent with his mom, a Christmas gift from the heart.

CRAFTY LADY

A Tribute by
Stephen Geez
StephenGeez.com
Image by Geez

"You *made* this?"
   Yes, she *made* that.

Mom had volunteered when my school's sixth-grade classes combined for one big holiday celebration before Christmas break. She and a handful of "room mothers" offered to share responsibility for decorations, snacks, and activities.

Of course, Mom came up with a little something extra.

She started by crocheting one palm-sized holiday wreath on a brass ring—layers of ruffly bright green studded with pinpoints of tiny glittery ornaments, pipe-cleaner-tip pine cones, and a festive red-ribbon bow. Pinning it to my sweater, she studied it thought-fully, mentally refined the execution, then proceeded to make several more. Some dozen or so wreaths into the project, it became clear she intended to make enough for every one of my school's hundred-plus eleven- and twelve-year-olds to have his or her own. Never doubting the girls would gush over them, I voiced concern that boys might consider them a bit too, um, un-cool. Mom just smiled and predicted they would like them, too, even if some opted to save them as gifts for their own mothers to wear.

The first few boys to receive their homemade wreaths eyed them suspiciously, yet quickly found them irresistible, deciding they really were, indeed, quite cool—but only if pinned to a pants-leg. Any placement of the more traditional variety—on the breast, sleeve, or even collar—well, that must have looked girly. Yes, "leg-wreaths" proved to be a guy thing, and while the girls admired each other's pretty ornaments, the boys strutted about, proudly showing off their macho holiday displays, grateful to "Aunt Lorene" or "Mrs. G" for her simple gift.

Still, what stood out to me that day, besides the pride of having the cool mom who put so much effort into making every youngster feel good, was the reaction of one quiet boy in particular, a lad whose name I've long since forgotten. As Mom pinned his very own wreath just above his left knee, he smiled shyly, big-eyed in amazement over such a thoughtful gesture. "You *made* this?" he whispered. "For *me?*"

I can't possibly recount how many times I've heard similar sentiments expressed in the years since. Most of the people who have passed through my mother's world now own a gift she made just for them. A master of all kinds of arts and crafts, known far and wide by the e-moniker "CraftyLady," Mom stands as the all-time master of melding utility with whimsy, of fitting function with the funnest of forms. Usually her own design, always cus-tom-made, her projects range from simple fridge-magnet knick-knacks to hand-carved saddles and clocks. My leather briefcase and desk set, the afghans gracing Loretta Lynn's home, baby clothes for friends and kin, dollies and frillies, wallets and belts, cozies and costumes—you name it, and Mom likely made it her-self.

You see, Mom understood something that day at the sixth-grade party, something I had only begun to learn. She knew those kids couldn't help but like their homemade wreaths, for even the too-coolest of any big little boy is smart enough to recognize that a gift from one's hands truly comes from the heart.

Those hand-crafted holiday trifles brought countless smiles to more than a hundred youngsters and their families, but I suspect that not more than a few, if any, are still around. Things don't last forever, just as mothers don't live forever.

We lost Mom on the saddest of days, the Ides of March in '08. Much of what she made is treasured by those she left behind, but what lives on is the gift she shared with us all. It's not so much the mere *things* she fashioned, but rather the smiles she coaxed, the caring she showed, the attention she shared. Mom filled our hearts with the art and craft of her love.

And even if you never met her, rest assured, she did make the world a happier place.

Yes, she *made* that.

For you.

MY BROTHER

A Tribute to a Murder Victim by
Stephen Geez
StephenGeez.com
Art by D.R. Wagner

I used to stand in my place in the stream, where one generation flows to the next, where lifetimes cascade from unseen sum-
mits to pool in the deep stillness that stretches beyond every
sunset, for there in the stream I could watch a single blossom float
by, and I would think of my brother and smile.

A few years behind me, a short ways up in the waters above,

he'd found his own good spot in the stream. Though not always able to see him, I could still feel when his words passed in the ripples, hear when his voice echoed from the trees, and laugh at the tales of so many travelers lucky enough to pass his way. Through it all, the waters kept washing around me, and I would know that my brother was there.

He's the one who always loved to watch things grow, a gardener at heart, a gentle man who would coax life from seedlings and dare magnificent flowers to flaunt their beauty for the world. And he's the one who always loved people, a friend at heart, a caring man who dared coax the best from all he touched. Yes, this I've seen, but with so many tales to tell, I know I'll never hear them all.

So I used to stand in my place in the stream, and think of my brother and smile.

But then on one of those brightest of days, the sky fell most wrenchingly dark, and the trees whispered of another man's pain lashing out blindly, an instant of cruel violence that never cared to learn its victim's name. I searched in vain at his place in the stream, but when the shadow had passed, my brother was gone.

I closed my eyes and wept, my tears mingling with those of so many who'd felt him slip beyond our grasp. And the waters churned fiercely, but I stood fast, if only because my brother had left me this moment at his place in the stream. For when I opened my eyes, there before me bloomed the most magnificent garden, and the people he loved had gathered to witness his work, and to promise we'll never forget.

My brother had left the world a better place, a remarkable legacy for one man in the short time he'd spent there at his own place in the stream. We'll *all* tend to his flowers, we vowed, and by remembering, we'll know he can't ever die.

So we stood in the stream and saw a mournful old flower drop a single blossom into the water. We all watched as it chased after my brother and disappeared into the deep pools of stillness that stretch beyond every sunset, there where our sister, his twin, had passed before us, a reminder the stream stops for no one, and that each place is ours but for a while.

Now I stand here again at my own place in the stream, and though my brother is gone, I remember he did find his own moments of joy, and he shared them with those who bothered to care.

So when a single blossom floats by, I'll think of him and smile, for I *do* know his name.

Gregory Dean was a *good* man, and I'll always be proud he was *my* brother.

TANYA'S KITE

A Tribute by
Stephen Geez
StephenGeez.com
Art by Geez

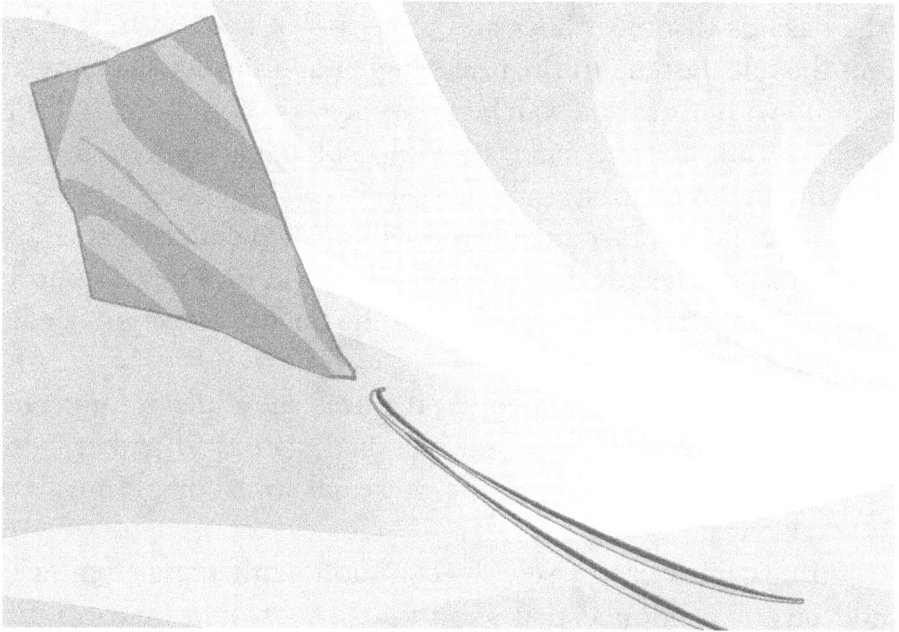

Springtime brings renewal. The countryside thaws, flowers and trees bud, and bitter cold yields to the warm gusts of a new summer in that inexorable reaffirmation of life. This is the time, when conditions are just right, for flying a kite.

Many springtimes ago my little sister, Tanya, saved her allowance and bought a kit for building one of these aeronautical wonders. Only about eight or nine at the time, she methodically assembled it without assistance or advice, then set it aside, anxiously monitoring the weather, waiting for the perfect day.

It arrived one afternoon when a patch of rain clouds drifted beyond the horizon to reveal azure sky, sunshine bathing our neighborhood in its warm glow, a steady breeze stirring from the south.

Tanya gathered every spare roll of string and twine she could find, then carried her prized pink diamond-flyer out to the driveway and launched it high. Navigating between tree-tops, avoiding the hazards of power lines and utility poles, she carefully played out the line, hoping to float hers higher and farther than any kite had flown before. She watched proudly as it continued to lift effortlessly into the air, her ersatz explorer tugging gently at its reins, seeking the freedom to sail where it may.

I loitered nearby, certainly too old for such childish games, but ready to help her tie another roll when the first played out. Of course I lingered for a while in case she might succeed in needing a third.

And still the kite climbed. By the time she added a fourth roll, an audience of neighborhood kids had started to gather, some contributing more string to the cause, all applauding Tanya's remarkable feat.

Mom came out to assess the commotion, then pulled me aside and quietly cautioned that soon the stress would be too much, that mere string would surely break and leave Tanya heartbroken. Still, to our little aeronaut, testing the limits of sky had proven more important than any certainty of retrieval.

I can't say how many rolls were pressed into service that day, but I do recall that kite fading so far into the distance that latecomers would need binoculars to confirm what we already knew.

One boy set out on his bicycle, pedaling furiously northward, returning later to confirm that Tanya's kite hovered in sight of the big cemetery with manicured lawns and a chapel and turtle pond, where geese gather to stand sentry over loved ones lost.

Eventually the sky darkened, the audience drifting away for suppers and television and bedtimes. It took quite a while, but Tanya, determined to bring the explorer home, managed to wind all that string and retrieve her great pink kite, remarkably intact and unscarred. If only that delicate assemblage of paper and wood and torn rags could share its glory, Tanya's would boast one of the finest kite tales ever told.

I don't know what happened to that kite. Our time with such ephemeral toys is inevitably short. Many are put away and forgotten, others broken or lost to those hazards that lurk at the fringes of everyday life. A few even manage to break free, never to be seen again, hopefully continuing their journeys on their own terms, in their own time.

In the coming years we learned to mark the advent of spring with Tanya's launch of each new kite. Sunny days offering brisk breezes would surely find her clutching a roll of twine, eyes to the distance, a rag-tailed flyer dancing against that vivid backdrop of blue. But even little girls grow up, and Tanya started having to fit her picnics and campouts and kite-flying jaunts between the demands of a busy career.

We especially cherished those rare trips to visit our parents at their home on a lake in the mountains. We'd go boating with Dad, and she'd lean out the bow, eyes closed, her arms catching the wind. We'd feed geese with Mom, and Tanya would gaze wistfully as eventually, inevitably, they would fly off to disappear against the blinding blue sky.

And she would cajole me into hiking with her to the natural bridge, climbing ridges until we towered over the valley, then pausing to watch cascading waterfalls crash into stair-step pools below. She always stood at the precipice and tilted her face up to the sun, and at those moments I knew that if I could give my sister anything in the world, it would be a magnificent pair of wings.

But like all seasons, springtimes must pass, and when Tanya was twenty-eight years old one of those hazards lurking at the edges of everyday life proved too much. The sun had set on a bitter winter day, and in the darkness her car skidded across a patch of black ice.

The string broke that night, and I lost my little sister, the beautiful young woman who loved animals and people, the little girl who never gave up, the magically buoyant soul who always found her wind.

Hundreds attended her funeral, a tribute from those lucky enough to have known and loved her. I don't think that warm spring day when she'd decided to fly her pretty pink kite was mentioned; so much had happened in the years since, too many poignant moments to recall.

She was buried there in the cemetery with the manicured lawns, close to the chapel and turtle pond, where geese gather to stand sentry over loved ones lost.

Some say death is a part of living, not a moment to fear. Hopes and dreams, no matter how big or small, give us the impetus to reach. There will always be risks and hazards inherent in all we try to achieve, in every place we venture, whenever we dare to share, and in those times we test the boundaries to see, if only for that moment, how it feels to soar. I'm proud that my sister always lived on her own terms, never afraid to play out a little more string, eternally reaching for the sky.

I miss you, Tanya, and that never changes as the years breeze ever faster by, even as the springtimes come and go in that inexorable reaffirmation of life. Your only tethers to this world now are the memories twined among the people whose hearts you touched, each contributing another roll.

I'll never let go of my end, so you fly as high and as far as you ever imagined. Bathe the world in your sunshine, and my love will be your wind.

Noteworthies

WILLOW FLY WITH ME?

An Essay by
Stephen Geez
StephenGeez.com
Art by Dizzy

Springtime across wide swaths of North America brings a bounty of bugs called willowflies—or mayflies or fishflies or, when they swarm by the gazillions, several other names best not used in polite company.

Avoiding the encyclopedic details, let's just agree they're delicate wisps with gossamer wings and double-stranded tails like fine thread. Harmless for their lack of bite or sting, not known to carry or spread any maladies, willowflies are generally uninterested in you or your busy lives. Fishermen and -women appreciate the rabid frenzy they incite among the most angler-coveted bait-biters, from sleek trout darting up cold swift streams to fat pan-sized bream schooling amid brush in warm glassy ponds; but to most of us familiar with the species, they're known for the short adult lives they lead.

Yes, the adult lifespan of these delicate wind-blown denizens is measured not in years or weeks, but in mere hours.

In this regard they are quite opposite the human race. We're known for the longest of childhoods, the better to fill our brains with the knowledge and skills and cultural memes needed to navigate our complex civilizations. Then we can reasonably expect our adulthoods to last another five decades or more.

Now, that leaves us with plenty of time to waste, no matter how goal-driven or productive we are. Even in that phase of life when we're most driven to add our own twigs to the family tree, we are able to reach beyond mere reproductive urges in order to seek deeply abiding emotional bonds, which is possible only because we have what the poets call "time enough for love."

The willowfly spends most of its life—its childhood—in the water. Eggs laid during the springtime lead to ravenous summer larvae that fatten during the fall before settling in to become pupal mud-slumberers during long cold winters. The warmth of springtime sets the ancient cycle into fast motion, when willowflies "hatch" and emerge as perfect imagos, drying quickly, then swarming in great clouds and gobbing every surface for miles, their very brief lives dedicated to mating, laying, and dying. Many have to settle for filling the bellies of fat toads and largemouth bass, but that role nevertheless helps more than enough of their brethren survive long enough to propagate the species.

Lots of people live that same kind of hurry.

One newspaper advice columnist reassures a young woman that she is not a total loser for failing to keep pace with her friends who all married and produced broods of two-point-four children by age 23. Sure, it would be nice to live long enough for a chance to pose as the eldest in one of those five-generation photos, but how fun would that be if it caps a lifetime of settling for Mr. Okay, or enduring a series of failed marriages to Ms. She-can-cook, Missy Lets-me-gamble, Senorita Anytime-I-want, and Widow Has-her-own-money. Willowflies, near as we can tell, don't care whom they "hook up" with.

I mean, when it's now or never, who's got the time to look around, or to hope love will find you?

My friend waited until she finally found the man she truly loved—just before they discovered he suffered a severe, life-threatening illness. Suddenly he wouldn't have qualified for that young missy writing to advice columnists. That man didn't fit any plan, but my friend married him anyway because she, well, she loved him—even though that meant spending their honeymoon across country at a clinic promising little more than a fading glimmer of hope, a place he ultimately never left, making her a widow after only two weeks.

Don't feel sorry for the willowfly because its life is so short. Feel sorry for it because it can never learn how to live in its short time.

Don't pity the young widow who found the man she loved right before watching helplessly as he slipped away, or the elderly bachelor who waits a lifetime to spy *the one* in a shawl-draped wheelchair across the assisted-living center rec-room. Do pity all those other souls who approach life like a willowfly, only to spend five decades or more feeding the relentless demands of abiding regret, wondering what they missed.

Step outside come springtime, and walk among the willow-flies. You'll find that one might just land on your arm and sit very still, its gossamer wings and double-stranded tail like fine thread stirring in the breeze. By then, it will have accomplished its only goal, and will be spending a few moments—its last moments—on a chance simply to rest.

I hope, my friends, that you all live long and productive lives. Still, even the longest-lived among us must eventually discover that our time here seems but an instant. However you choose to spend yours, just remember how lucky you are. You can achieve what a willowfly will never know.

Don't squander this chance, for you have been blessed with the most precious gift:

Time enough for love.

HARDLY-CAP ZONE

An Essay by
Stephen Geez
StephenGeez.com
Art by Dizzy

My friend Mary runs a group home whose residents include a young woman in a wheelchair, her disabilities substantial. Still, nobody can slow her down—nor shut her up. When she's not working on projects, she's planning new ones, involving others, sharing her zeal. She exemplifies but one approach to dealing with handicap challenges.

Some of us are born with physical limitations, congenital differences we might never notice if not for observing those around us who are differently abled. Others are born within that range we call "normal," but then symptoms of encroaching maladies and syndromes—especially the biggies such as MD and ALS—diminish our capabilities. Still others suffer physical trauma, usually in an accident, leading to debility that is either temporary or permanent, or falls into that middle range where there is some improvement but not full recovery. Whether our handicaps are congenital, symptomatic, or traumatic tends to affect how we deal with them.

If we are born with what in a less-sensitive era were called "birth defects," we achieve our self-awareness having known ourselves no other way. While that might lead to frustration, resentment, or any number of coping mechanisms from hostility to acceptance, the difference is integral to each individual's self-image. Many succeed in developing compensatory capabilities such as enhanced hearing in lieu of sight, or powerful arms to compensate for incapable legs. Many, too, nurture optimism that someday medical science will positively affect their capabilities, maybe through stem-cell regrowth, cochlear implants, or whatever.

Those among us with encroaching debility that is symptomatic at least have the benefit of an adjustment period. Rather than having always been present, the limitations are something recognized to be oncoming, often in incremental stages. While I suspect nobody can truly be "ready," at least the period of mental and physical adaptation is drawn out over time, perhaps a bit easier to face, an opportunity to share those stages with loved ones and professionals who are expert in coping and preparing.

The sudden, usually accidental, sometimes unexpectedly tangential injury-caused handicaps nearly always catch victims by surprise. Sudden and jolting, the trauma is sometimes compounded by the ache of knowing others were also hurt—or worse. We know right away that certain wounds will cause permanent loss, but most involve at least an element of hoping for improvement through that age-old process of assessment, monitoring, treatment, healing, and rehabilitation. No matter how sudden the initial harm, we can still generally expect a period of adjusting to the new reality in tandem with gradually determining what that reality might be.

My own handicap followed the latter pattern: follow-up assessments after an accident during my college years predicted increasing debility as I aged. While I had hoped for better, I cannot claim surprise that I suffered deterioration, re-injury, inevitable surgery, and necessary lifestyle adjustments. I walk with a cane now, sometimes able to move fairly well, sometimes enduring periods of further limitation. During the ups, I push limits as much as I can, riding the exercise bike, even leaving the cane behind for short, manageable distances. In those instances, I often find people asking, "Why don't you use your cane?" My response:

"I'm trying to get better."

I do try to avoid making use of the various forms of handicap assistance that many have no choice but to accept. Unless I absolutely can't handle it that day, I prefer to stand in line with everyone else. Handicap parking is for having no other way to get to the store, not for someone who can easily make it from the back of the lot and probably should in order to reap the plusses of exercise.

I definitely notice substantial differences in attitudes among the differently abled. Where some resist that wheelchair with every bit of obstinance they can muster, finally sitting only with the attitude that they can't wait to get up and out of it soon; others seize that opportunity for relief, and you can just tell that once they sit, they'll never get up. Rehab therapists see the difference: some patients forestall every effort, every technique, every assistance toward getting better, their minds set on avoiding the frustration and pain that reminds them of their new limitations. Others arrive steeled with determination that can and will help them achieve what appear to be near miracles. And if they cannot succeed, even in part, they seem to find greater acceptance in knowing they did all they could, that they left no possibilities untested.

Much as I would like to preach the rewards of a positive attitude, nobody can know what works best for another without having lived his challenges. I have two close friends who write books, both suffering serious neurological debilities that interfere substantially with their work. One is so discouraged that he has virtually given up, even with several novels essentially finished but for the touch-ups. The other is undergoing brain surgery today that is very risky, even potentially fatal. In the run-up to this courageous act, he hustled admirably, finishing several major nonfiction projects, keeping me busy with editing and feedback, even during the difficult periods when he needed help remembering what he'd done, what still needed his attention. Maybe the first friend is better off for reducing the stress and pressure, but what I like about the other's approach is his conviction that he has much to say, and that extraordinary effort in the face of adversity is the only way to get his ideas said. He embodies the advice poet Dylan Thomas gave his father, who was losing his sight:

"Rage, rage against the dying of the light."

Our bodies can drag down our minds, but our minds have unlimited potential to uplift our bodies.

Medical science has clearly demonstrated a mind-body link in the promotion of healing. The right attitude can also help sustain us through our darkest challenges. When we know we will come no further, the right attitude can help us adjust to our new reality. I wonder if paradigm-shattering physicist Stephen Hawking would have achieved greatness in understanding our physical world had he not worked so much harder than the rest of us to assert the most rudimentary control over his own body's ability to function within it.

I can't do everything I used to, but I can use today's moments of difficulty as this opportunity to talk to *you*. That's no hike in the mountains, but it is quite cool, if not better in many ways.

If you face physical disability, do everything in your power to overcome it, from getting better to learning to live better with what you can never improve. Help resentment, blame, depression, and anger run their course so you get on with appreciating what's left, your own unique chance to discover renewed purpose.

If you are declining, get serious about prioritizing, then get busy, and don't be bashful about asking for help . . . or helping others.

The young woman in Mary's group home figured that out.

If life puts you in a wheelchair, don't look around for a place to park yourself . . .

Strap on a rocket and get rollin'!

HOW OLD, INDEED

An Essay by
Stephen Geez
StephenGeez.com
Image by Geez

"I sure wish I had put some trees in *my* yard," my neighbor said,
watching me trim branches on the row of flowering crabapples

that liked to reach over the sidestreet walkway and tickle the noggins of passersby.

Only a year into grad school and working full-time, I had just commenced one of those long-term projects called a "mortgage." Yes, I had bought my own place, a nice corner-lot colonial in a well-seasoned, thirty-year-old neighborhood. My house's original owners had planted enthusiastically, blessing me with gloriously mature flora: springtime bloomers such as apple, cherry, and crabs; robust blossom-gobbed shrubbery the likes of lilac, snowball, and forsythia; plus a towering trio of magnificent hot-summer shaders—a red maple that ended every sentence with "eh?"; the mischievous elm that liked to flirt with my grapevine; and a humongous cottonwood that could target any area swimming pool with a fusillade of silky white puffs, then laugh about it for days. My neighbor's yard, a mower-cropped crew-cut of featureless green, looked forlorn in comparison.

"Today's as good a day as any to plant a few," I pointed out.

He chuckled as if I'd made a joke, then shook his head and said, "Naw, it takes a good ten years or more till they're big enough to sit under."

I thought of him some years later when I saw an elderly woman interviewed on the news. Posing proudly in her cap and gown, she beamed over realizing her dream of going to college, four years of determined effort culminating in a bachelor's degree. When the interviewer asked about encouragement from friends and family, the elder-grad surprised me by admitting, "They all thought I was *nuts*." She said that when she enrolled, her grandson quickly pointed out she'd be 74 by the time she graduated. Her response still resonates with me today:

"And how old will I be in four years if I *don't* go to college?"

How old, indeed.

The very nature of a human lifespan presents life-plan challenges. Nearly all of us have reliable data on when our individual clocks started ticking—it's right on the birth certificate—but except in rare instances, we have only a vague notion of now much time we'll get to live and love, to laugh and learn. That's why we try to cram so many accomplishments into our younger days. I mean, the sooner you achieve a goal, the more time you'll have to enjoy the benefits.

However, this perspective is rather outcome-oriented. At the lower level in a hierarchy of ambition, we choose quick-and-simple aims, the kind where we expect lesser efforts to produce quicker results. At the middle level, we pursue the kinds of substantial rewards that require long-term, sustained effort—which in turn imbues success with greater meaning. At the highest level, we work toward goals where the benefits extend beyond our time, service to future generations, a paying forward for what our forebears accomplished for us. Imagine the old-timer who patiently plants a thousand seed-lings, knowing he'll never live to see the forest, a form of altruism too few of us ever learn to embrace. Failing to see our world and the people who share it as bigger than one individual—as a continuum enduring beyond a single lifetime—is how it comes to seem acceptable to ignore the long-term consequences of pollution and climate change, of rapid natural-resource depletion, of amassing a massive collective debt for future generations to pay down.

Maybe we don't always need a "result." The old lady didn't say her goal was a degree, but rather "to go to college." If she ran out of time after a year or two or three, wouldn't the experience, the knowledge, the mere accomplishment found in *effort* be worth it? If you plant a tree, won't watching it grow, if only for a while, offer a measure of satisfaction? Don't the best destinations beckon us with the promise of a meaningful journey?

And can't the results of our best efforts prove different than we expect, maybe even better, with dividends paying in more ways than we ever imagined? Think about the never-too-late lesson younger generations learn from the example set by that elderly college coed. Think about the circle-of-life wonder a child discovers when an old-timer nurtures seedlings that will mature long after he's gone.

And even if nobody ever finds out what *you* have done, at least you can embrace the joy in knowing you've made yourself a better person, and you've left the world better for the time *you* got to live and love, to laugh and learn.

It's been a long time since I lived among those springtime bloomers, blossom-gobbed shrubs, and towering trio of magnificent hot-summer shaders; but I hope my former neighbor is still right there across the street, and that he did get around to planting those trees. I like to imagine him spending some golden-years time relaxing in the shade. But if he's gone now, I expect his son inherited the house, and I hope that on a hot summer day *he* can sit in that shade with his own children and share memories about helping his dad plant those trees.

How old do you have to be to understand that such a simple result is worth all that effort?

How old, indeed.

OPPOSITES ATTACH

An Essay by
Stephen Geez
StephenGeez.com
Image by Geez

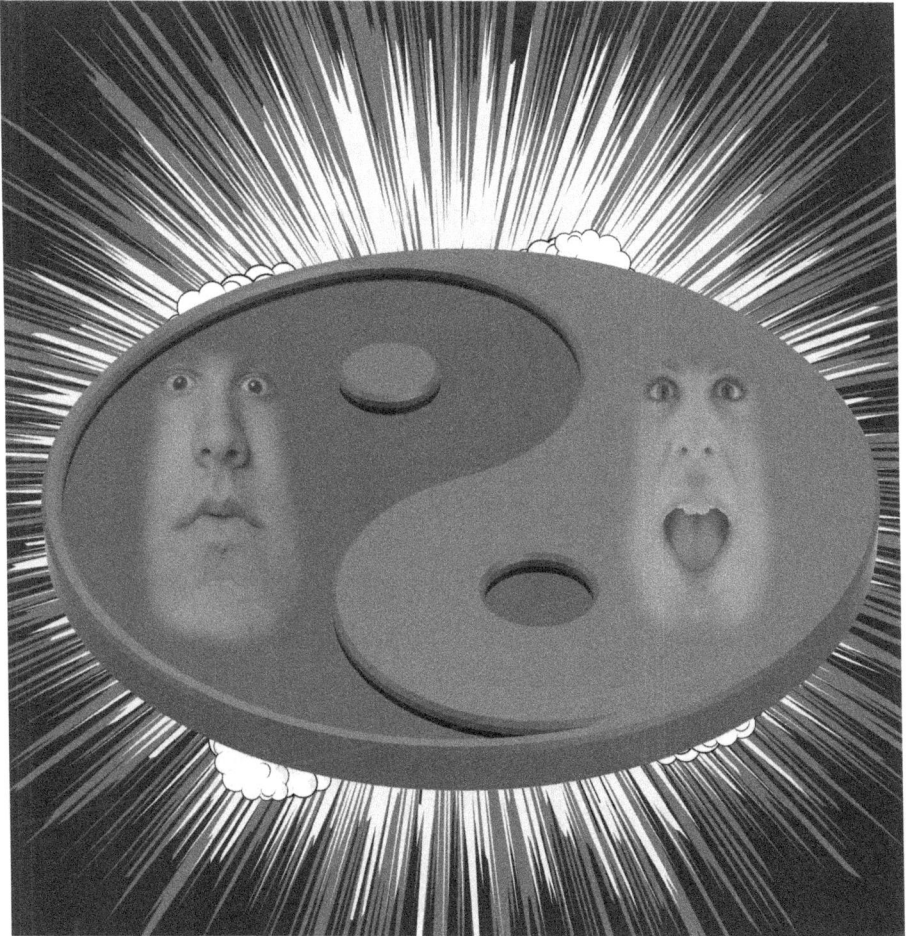

Compatibility is not always about two yins in sync. After all, sometimes opposites attach.

Used to be, I'd travel long distance to visit my parents for the occasional long weekend, and I'd maximize my quality time by indulging both Mom's yin and Dad's yang. See, Dad's m.o. has always been that darkness signals sleepy time—can't be staying up too much later—and the first glimmers of day breaking over the horizon mean you've overslept. I've long lived more in sync with Mom's circadian pattern: night is for staying up late, while the first few hours of daylight are for those early birds and the clueless worms they crave.

After dark is when my energy kicks in, and if I'm working on a project, I can go and go and go until the cows come home, until they've rested for the night, even until they've headed out for the morning shift. With minimal distraction and fewer interruptions, night is the best part of the day.

So during my visits Dad would trundle off to bed by ten, and I'd stay up till the wee hours with Mom, usually at the dining-room table, "catching up." Then I'd sleep for a few hours and drag my carcass out of bed in time to join my impatient father for some serious daybreak bass-fishing. This worked quite well: day-times all together, quality one-on-one time in the wee hours, "wee" covering the early wees as well as the late wees.

All couples have at least some big differences in the way they live, their comfort zones, their likes and dislikes. Mom would look at any old useless thing and see something she could make from it, so she'd put it aside and eventually use it. Dad's more the type who thinks everything not currently in use should be tossed out. I mean, if you're not holding it *in your hand*, the second you look away it's gone.

Think of the ways people you know manage to mesh when they don't, you know, *mesh*. Think of examples with yourself.

Some aren't comfortable unless their living area is fully lit, every nook and cranny bright. I like it darker, moody, with pools of soft light only where I need to see, fluorescence not worth the squint.

Have you seen one party wince when a sound blaster takes charge of the music or television? It's likely the same one who thrives on commotion, quick to invite the crowd over, kids and all. Notice that someone else will quietly slip out for some alone time.

Some are uncomfortable in sterile neatness, any space lacking a homey lived-in-ness; while others can't stand to ignore the universal truth of a place for everything and *Would you please put everything in its place?!*

I can't stand to wear uncomfortable clothing, but I know people who would don acid-infused cactus-thorn barb-wire knit if they thought it made them look good.

I have one friend who really ought to wear a holster for his combs because the world is full of mirrors, and he simply cannot pass one without a quick-draw touch-up lest a single obstinate strand stray from the fold. Others consider their hairstyles one of the fun intrigues of life—ain't no telling what they'll see next time a mischievous mirror coaxes a look.

I have a cousin whose checkbook balance one time had the gall to be a penny off. She found the error, eventually, and made it regret ever hiding from her. I'll bet you know people who aren't even sure what they can spend those last weeks before a monthly statement arrives.

Ever seen an indoors-type homebody fall in love with an outdoors-type nature lover? I guess they can make it work by meeting up at a window every now and then.

I know a guy who subscribes to three different television guides for efficiently planning preferred viewing with the least time investment and the best chances of never missing priorities. Ever hang ten with a remote-control surfer? Have these types *ever* seen the beginning of a movie or show?

You know how many celebratory receptions I've attended

with a loved one who can boogie all night to little more than the sound of a ringing doorbell? As a musician, I prefer to dance with my fingers and my mind. My caboose prefers to sit.

Watch a couple of old married coots and figure out which one always knows what time it is, the date, *the year*, as well as where they're supposed to be, and when. Odds are, the other is clueless—and it doesn't matter as long as one is keeping track for both.

Often one partner is intensely private while the other just cannot understand why everybody and his dog shouldn't know all of their personal business.

On foot, in a car, strapped to jet engines . . . if I'm here and need to get there, I'm on a mission, look out!, *vrocm vroom*; yet I'm probably stuck traveling with someone who considers it sufficient to show a bit of hazy intent to sort of move in the intended direction at some point more or less—or not. I mean, who wants to road-trip with a pokey who needs to examine every item in the Cracker Barrel gift shop when I'm already frustrated that bathroom breaks require bringing the rolling vehicle to a full stop?

Some couples prefer to sit close together at dinner because one will snarf anything that's not still moving while the other eats almost nothing—and then only if it's prepared just the right way, and isn't touching the other items.

A night away from home? One is sorely disappointed by three-star service in the restaurant at a four-star hotel; the other sees no tragedy in forgetting to bring the grill-grate to a campout, seeing as how there are plenty of sticks to sharpen, just jab that slab of meat and hang it over the fire.

Who else would a safety nut marry if not a consummate risk-taker? Isn't the fact of their marriage a risk?

Some people despise animals and can't fathom why others would bring them into the house. That's a spouse in the making for some Doolittle who owns one or two pets of every stripe, plus some quirky species of beast nobody's ever fully identified, the one that just gave birth to a huge brood of squirmies.

I know someone who goes into panic mode if the gas gauge dips down close to half full. She's married to a guy who sees no reason to stop as long as he can swerve back and forth and slosh some drops and a bit of fumes into the injector.

I could go on with examples—I even started a list that got way too long for one short essay—but what matters, in my humble estimation, is that somehow we muddle through and make it work. Or at least we should. Maybe too many don't, and that's sad in itself.

You see, too often in life we face the wrenching jolt of losing the one we love, after which those differences don't seem to matter so much anymore. I get cold easily, preferring the heat high, covers thick, air toasty; yet I miss someone quite the opposite. Really, subject her to a night with the room temp above sixty and she might well spontaneously combust. I seem to recall that she actually did once—combust, I mean.

Mom's been gone a few years now. Our times together to "catch up" have passed. Dad still gets up in time to taunt the intrepid largemouth bass, but when he goes to bed early every night, the house falls quiet.

Appreciate your differences, and appreciate the ones you care about all the more because of those differences. Don't expect compatibility always to be about two yins in sync.

You might just fall in love with a yang.

THE SKINNY ON FAT

An Essay by
Stephen Geez
StephenGeez.com
Art by Joe Posada

I once knew a pretty girl . . .

My age, eleven or twelve, with long silky hair and a sweet smile, Sherry Woodcock lived around the block from me. I rode my bike to see her one day, a nice visit, lots of chances for me to make her laugh, but then she said something I didn't like. Making fun of my being so skinny, she quipped, "You look like you could just blow away in the wind."

Sure, years earlier worrisome adults had expressed some concern about my low-weight physique, but the doc assured everyone of my healthiness.

I spent much of my childhood encouraged to eat as much as I could possibly want, but I kept so active that I managed to strike the precise balance between calories in and calories burned. After the Sherry quip, I tried harder to gain weight, even worked out with barbells for a year or so, but I never found any way to add even an ounce of fat or an inch of bulk. Over six feet tall by ninth grade, I boasted a waspy 28" waist that stayed at 28" well into my thirties. I fondly recall the sheer joy in Mom's face when a marathon session of school-clothes shopping paid off by ferreting out that extremely rare pair of pants with men's inseams and a boys' waistline.

We live in a world where more than two-thirds of all adults want to lose weight. We have grown a huge industry of services, products, systems, facilities, and motivational message-mongering to promote the shedding of pounds and encourage keeping them off. Common now are enterprises offering diet plans that include purchasing their own proprietary weight-managing foods. It is a mark of promotional genius that these companies advertise weight-loss assistance by tempting prospects with enticing images of artfully photographed, fully prepared gourmet-caliber meals.

In many ways, the drive to eat is unique among our most dominant of biological imperatives. It is a deeply imbedded and recurring desire that one has no choice but to indulge. We eat, or we die, the latter option including rather unpleasant sickness, weakness, and decline as part of the painful process. Indulging provides double reinforcement.

It reduces discomfort—rather like satisfying our needs for shelter and temperature; and it provides pleaure—much like that nifty drive to procreate. In fact, we have raised the preparation of food to the level of fine art.

The imperative to consume water carries greater urgency, but even though we have made the creation of potables an art form, too, we can be perfectly satisfied surviving on plain, unadulterated water. Try that with a food diet based entirely on dry cakes of burlap-flavored fiber or bowls of slime-infused nutri-soylent.

The important difference between food and water, though, is that our bodies are well equipped to store food energy long-term, while our water reserve is good for about a day or two before we start depleting our operating supply. We are hard-wired to eat more than our immediate needs as a hedge for long-term survival during downturns in our food resources. Therefore, because our bodies want us to eat more while the eatin' is good, and since our minds reinforce this behavior by reducing discomfort and in-creasing pleasure, most of us live like we're facing famine when in reality citizens of any prosperous society never need to eat more than their daily requirements. Unless you live at the fringes, or enjoy a lifestyle requiring reserves—say, as a mountain climber or marathon runner—you likely eat too much, too often.

This leads to problems compounded by two major factors: the foods we eat, and the metabolisms we rely on to process them.

Never have our foods packed so much energy into every bite, our diets saturated with carbs and fats in seemingly infinite variety of textures and flavors, available in vast quantities, widely acces-sible, amazingly affordable. Granted, our options for healthful choices are increasing, but we do need to be vigilant in protecting our right to make our own choices. I believe government inter-vention has its place in protecting the integrity and safety of our food supply, in reducing scourges such as microbial contamina-tion and toxin adulteration; but sin-taxing Mountain Dew or barring McDonald's from offering toys with Happy Meals pushes way too far into what some call "The Nanny State." Our species succeeded wildly in the quest for maintaining reliable sources of sustenance; we just need to improve our overall ability to manage that success.

Metabolisms play a key role in most obesity problems, too—as many a frustrated overweight dieter will attest. Body types that are very efficient at storing fat once offered a survival plus. Given that now most people never want for food, those same metabolisms act as a survival minus, turning higher odds of triumphing over famine into lower odds of living long with diabetes and heart disease. Many experts believe this is the main reason our once-steady increase in life expectancy has largely stalled; advances in medical science helping more of us survive ever more maladies are being offset by widening obesity-related health declines.

Sherry making fun of me left me feeling bad. Still, even at that age, I already felt even worse for my fat friends, some of whom I knew ate less than I even while adding inches to their waistlines. While some skinnies are quick to assume an obese person is merely a glutton with no self-control, I have long known that this is often nowhere near the truth.

Complicating the challenge of preventing excess weight gain, our bodies adjust their food needs much as they adjust to the presence of substances that cause addiction. Many overweight people have raised the bar, so to speak, on their nutritional needs, which increases both the discomfort from *not* eating at the higher level while also increasing the pleasure that comes from satisfying it. Someone who has been too heavy since childhood faces a substantially greater challenge in adjusting his or her metabolism than someone who only recently added some excess pounds. Hence, childhood obesity has become such a big concern because those youngsters can likely expect a greater struggle, too often for life.

Much has been written about the role of our increasingly

sedentary lifestyles. Fewer of us are burning substantial amounts of calories earning a living and enjoying our leisure-time activities. Worse, many reach the tipping point where being bigger and having less energy makes it harder to work and play, especially when weight-related debility factors in with the likes of bad joints, heart and circulation problems, diminished lung capacity, and more.

It's difficult to make a lot of money selling the best system for reducing obesity: 1) Eat smart and less, and 2) Exercise smarter and more. For youngsters, we need to shape their lives to encompass this maxim. We also must ensure that the adults they emulate model the same approach to caring for one's body.

If you're already too big and, worse, getting bigger, do whatever it takes to wrestle your weight back under your own control. Maybe look into those plans advertising scrumptious weight-plan foods; they seem to be effective for many. Learn by reading, watching, talking—whatever it takes to understand how your body operates and what possible ideas you might discover for enhancing its health. Discover how exercise really can be fun, not just drudge-work. Discover that health-smart foods really can be tasty, not just bland and unfilling. Don't stop trying until you find the combination of healthful eating and healthful living that works for you.

My cousin Lendia is one of my heroes for doing what it takes. Too many factors conspired against her, including inheriting a challenging metabolism. She worked long and hard at controlling her weight, but when it became clear that diet and exercise would not suffice, when her health began to suffer exponentially, she bravely opted for surgical intervention. Risky, painful, temporarily debilitating, her choice required a period of being dependent on others, sacrificing her penchant to be the loving soul who looks out for everyone else. Bless her heart, she has since shed well over 100 pounds. She feels good, looks great, enjoys rapidly improving mobility and health, and now expects to be with us longer, all the while enjoying a greater quality of life.

Pay attention: That list of benefits Lendia earned, those can be *your* rewards, the positive reinforcements that outweigh reducing the discomfort of hunger by enjoying the fleeting pleasure of fattening foods:

Look good.

Feel better.

Move freer.

Live longer.

Here's the greatest reward of all: giving that gift to the youngsters you love means they will also look good, feel better, move freer, and live longer. That's a payoff bigger than your own, the kind you pass along, one that will outlast even your lifetime.

Me, I'm in fairly good shape, though I could lose twenty pounds.

I wish my accidental handicap didn't seriously curtail my much-loved activities such as scuba-diving and long-distance river canoeing, the kinds of regular pastimes that use to keep me svelte and, well, ruggedly handsome. I'm astounded by the notion that I once wished I could *gain* weight, and that I could ever let someone make me feel bad for being slim and healthy. Heck, I must have fared well in the years after my visit around the block; I never did just blow away in the wind.

I have no idea what became of Sherry. I do hope the girl who teased me about being thin hasn't grown unhealthy and fat. If she has a slender grandson who finds himself wishing he could gain weight, surely she would hug him and tell him to count his blessings, that it's more about taking care of yourself than worrying about what anybody else thinks of your appearance.

She might even have a story to tell him:

"I once knew a skinny boy . . ."

SOMEONE I LOVE QUIT SMOKING

An Essay by
Stephen Geez
StephenGeez.com
Art by Dizzy

Someone I love quit smoking.

What a great cause for celebration! Whenever anybody you

care about quits, you should consider that a momentous occasion, too.

Too bad our culture doesn't offer an elaborate ritual to acknowledge such a life-affirming transition, just as it does for births, marriages, retirements, and so on. Sure, some quitters eventually stop quitting, but I'm fairly certain more than a few marriages eventually fail, too. No amount of pomp and ceremony guarantees any commitment will never come undone, but smoke-stoppers deserve our encouragement, and maybe sincere demonstrations of heartfelt recognition will help them persist that all-important little bit more.

I started losing people to smoke—and witnessing firsthand how wrenchingly they suffered in decline—during my undergrad years, which also happened to be when I got my first book contract: an overview of addiction prevention and treatment methodology. I researched and analyzed virtually every program and study from around the world to identify the best. Back then, the nascent tobacco-cessation movement had barely started; it would be many years before the advent of packaged systems and aids like nicotine patches and gums.

Still, much of what I learned holds true today: quitting cold turkey tends to prove more successful than gradual weaning; all it takes is one completely smoke-free month to quell nicotine-with-drawal symptoms; and if weaning is to work, acute awareness of the triggers helps focus resolve on moments of vulnerability. Simply waiting thirty minutes after cues such as eating, coffee-breaking, or waking up helps sever those links that urge smokers to smoke. Determination, though, and a keen understanding of the stakes in failure, these matter most. After all, nearly all smokers eventually want very much to quit, but many need help.

I never advocate curtailing anyone's civil liberties, nor do I subscribe to the notion of controlling others' behaviors through onerous regulation or excessive taxation. I do agree with reasonable limits in the public square, fair opportunity for smokers to smoke along with freedom for the rest of us not to breathe it.

I'm a fan of Dr. Joseph R. DiFranza of the University of Massachusetts Medical School in Worcester. A researcher devoting much of his career to understanding tobacco addiction, he has shown how one in ten adolescents experience symptoms within two days of their first smoke. That rate rises to one in three within a month. A large New Zealand study finds one in four symptomatic within their *first four cigarettes*. Dr. DiFranza cites cases where the *first cigarette* affected one's brain enough to trigger the onset of addiction. His model explains how the cravings signal more than a desire to avoid withdrawal; rather, the brain has altered its biochemical makeup to accommodate the ongoing presence of nicotine. Quitters aren't just learning to go without; they're struggling to change back into what they used to be.

Into what they were *meant* to be.

Okay, so that makes me a big fan of the whole *Don't Start* school of thought, but many we love have already been smoking for a long time. It begins in response to social conditioning, maybe owing a bit to advertising, certainly owing a lot to peer pressure. I'm most sympathetic to those who started before we really knew the danger, before those who did know were forced to admit how harmful smoking really is. That's when my loved one got addicted, but for anyone starting today there simply is no excuse.

What everybody ought to know by now is simple: tobacco smoke is the method of drug ingestion that often proves fatal when used as directed. It diminishes one's ability to survive, and to live productively and pain-free. Yeah, sure, a rare few manage to reach "old age" despite smoking, but I'll bet they could have lived even longer. Smoking severely damages a body, and the sooner one quits, the better the odds at least some of that damage can be reversed.

I'm proud of the many I've known who simply chose to live longer, healthier lives, then steeled their determination. Others quit because they had to—each new smoke started causing severe respiratory distress; hospital rules forbade lighting up in the cancer ward; open flame carried the risk of igniting an oxygen tank . . . If you haven't quit while you could still breathe, odds are you will when you're gasping for every breath.

And yet, my good friend's mother, three years into fighting lung and related cancers—surgeries, chemo, radiation—still sneaks smokes, thinking nobody knows.

Choosing to start smoking, choosing to quit—these are not decisions you make only for yourself. Does anybody love you? Seriously, we all have acquaintances, many we call friends, but who is on that list of people who truly love you?

What in life would be harder for them to face than watching you die?—especially knowing it didn't have to happen, that you chose for them years of your own fading relevance, that you opted out of sticking around long enough to see how it all turns out?

I've had smokers tell me everybody's gotta die of *something*. Oh yeah? But when? And how? And with how much quality of life at the end?

It hurts more than you can imagine to think of the people I've loved already dead by smoke. Plus, I have to deal with knowing that to this day my best friend continues to smoke, as do the majority of my closest friends. I've tried, and I intend to keep trying, but I can't make them stop.

After all that research, I still don't know how.

So now I'm going to write it out:

If you're not already a smoker, please don't start. I keep hearing that it's really hard to quit.

If you do smoke, please stop. Care enough about yourself, and think about who in this vast world loves you, then decide how much you're willing to hurt them.

If someone *you* love smokes, please don't pretend it's okay. At least try pointing out that you're worth quitting for. It might just work. If not, maybe it'll be easier to live with the loss knowing you tried.

And finally, if you can't find the right words, you're welcome to use mine.

The one I love smoked for a long time. She did try to quit on a number of occasions, and one day she finally succeeded. She learned how to live smoke-free, something she could have done long ago, even when she thought she couldn't.

As proud and grateful as I am for what she did, though, the sad fact is that when too much damage is done, quitting can only buy you a bit more time.

I wanted more, way more than the little bit she got.

And I know it never should have ended that way.

Yes, someone I love quit smoking . . .

Too late.

DONKEY-BALLIN'

An Essay by
Stephen Geez
StephenGeez.com
Art by Turtle

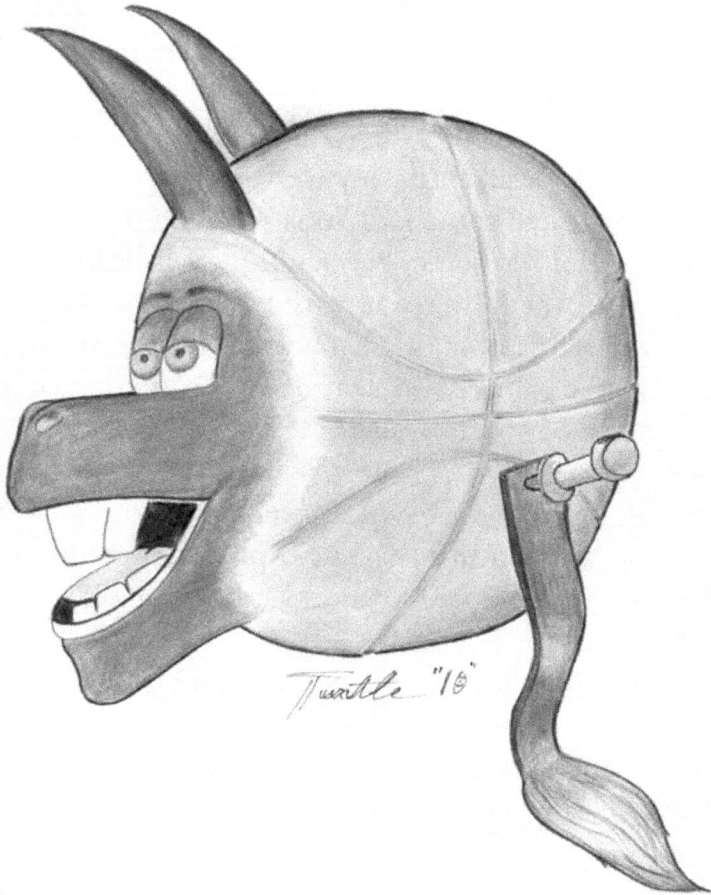

I'm trying to get some projects done today, but I seem to be distracted by a hankering to watch a good ol' game of donkey basketball.

That's right. For clarity, and to tweak those search engines, I'll say it again:

Donkey basketball.

I figure to have been about seven years old the first time I watched some real-live donkey basketball. Cousin Tommy treated me to a game in the local high-school gym—a charity event, I think. It proved quite the paradigm-shifting experience. Used to be, in the '60s and '70s, you could find a rip-roaring donkey game every now and then, and although that's still possible, it's a bit of a rarity nowadays.

I'm not sure about the origin of the concept, nor do I feel a burning need to research it, but I imagine there's quite a story behind the first time somebody took a notion to introduce a bit of the old hee-haw to the noble tradition of b-ball. Let's just say everybody really ought to see it played at least once in a lifetime.

Donkey basketball is not what you might picture; the animals don't dribble the ball or shoot baskets, no matter how impressive their repertoire of sporting skills. They don't appear to be very motivated, either. I doubt your average donkey aspires to earn fame and adulation, the big paydays, a long career in the endorsement industry. Rather, it's *people* who play the game, each teammate sitting astride his very own jackass—or she-ass, I suppose, a detail I'm not sure matters.

Watching is fun because the donkey can be counted on to do only one thing—well, two, if you include that mess plopping all over the floor. You see, apparently each donkey is tasked with the role he does best, which is *not* to cooperate with the intentions of his unwelcome cohort.

Picture the frustrated donkey-rider: "All right! I've got the ball! Let's drive to the basket! Let's go—just drive to the basket! C'mon, let's—hey! No, not that way. Where you going? We're playing this end. Hey, why'd you stop? What are you—? Oh cripe, don't do that here—ugh, *what did you eat?*"

Yeah, it's a real hoot to watch the unfolding drama, but to those frustrated, mission-thwarted players, that donkey can be a real ass.

So I found myself there in the gym at the big-kids' school, as thoroughly entertained by all the floor-plopping as any typical seven-year-old, thinking that something about this doesn't quite make sense. I mean, why ride the donkey? Just get off it and go take the shot. Seriously.

Eventually one player did just that—or tried. See, he didn't watch where he stepped. The way he wound up proved quite the sight, sitting there in . . . well, let's just say the shot sailed wide. Just as well, because it wouldn't have counted. Even donkey-ball has rules, rather like the game of life. If you want to score, you should *play* by the rules, no matter how many jackasses you have to deal with.

So how do those determined players cope with the challenges and limitations of riding stubborn brayers? They develop strategies. They learn to flip a leg over and play side-back, or turn around and ride backwards. They sharpen their passing skills, increase their reliance on savvy teamwork. They abandon all notions of individual hot-dogging in favor of a rather haphazard form of zone offense. You see, possessing the ball isn't quite as important as striving for the best placement, so if you can get your donkey to wander anywhere near your opponents' basket, your job is to keep him there until the ball comes to you.

Be ready to take your shot.

Life is like that, too—working with what you got, respecting the rules, and overcoming impediments so you can maneuver to the best place at the right time, ready to take your shot.

The older I get, the more I find myself dismayed by the lack of follow-through from those around me claiming ambition they seem unbothered to pursue. It's like they pass their days lingering idly on the back of some donkey, when really they could achieve more.

They sabotage themselves, make the job unnecessarily hard, refuse to turn themselves around and sight the goal. They join forces with contrary cohorts, let themselves be led the wrong way, count on others who don't really care.

Sometimes those rules do make the game especially difficult, our limitations unduly cumbersome, our goals seeming to recede into the distance, our teammates unable to help. Still, we smile, bear down, and get to work.

Sure, playing life's game from the back of a donkey can be quite fun . . . but only for a little while.

You see, if you truly want to get something done, sometimes you just need to get off your ass.

Oh, and watch where you step.

BE THE BOX

An Essay by
Stephen Geez
StephenGeez.com
Art by Dizzy

Think outside the box.

Yeah, I know, it's rather cliché, the old shift-your-paradigm adage. This sage advice is delivered more often than not by some-one too comfortable inside the box to do his own outside think-ing, better to let *you* take all the risk. Too many of those chanting outside-the-box mantras forget to open the lid and truly learn what's inside.

Much as I like to prattle metaphorically, I must admit a lifelong affinity for the literal incarnation of these cubist devices. Crafted of myriad materials from cardboard to mahogany to platinum, boxes represent one of the greatest inventions, a physical way to hold "stuff" every bit as efficiently as figurative boxes hold "ideas." Once I've emptied a box, I find it hard to discard. I mean, look, it's a perfectly good box; and one of those certainties in life is that at some point sooner than later, we all need another box.

Kids are quick to recognize potential in the box itself, their innocent indifference to expectation a state of grace that too many outgrow as they hurtle toward adulthood and all that inside-the-box versus outside-the-box thinking. Why, just turn that crank, and maybe this go-round Jack will jump right out of the box—or will he? How many times have you seen a kid put aside his birthday present, then opt to play with the box? Look!—it's a fort, a roller-coaster rocket, an unrealized diorama to host min-iature fantasy realms, the perfect turbo-sled to zoom down that Little League World Series hill, Captain Jack's time-capsule and treasure-chest transmogrificationator . . .

Then when you grow up and the world demands your earnest contributions, go ahead and try to think outside the box, if you want, but make sure to remember . . . it's just a box. Maybe it contains precisely what you think you want, mail-ordered and de-livered to your door. It might sport festive wrap and tease you with the most amazing gift from someone you love. It might very well cradle a lifetime's cherished mementos hidden in some dusty attic, or the meager belongings of a gentle soul who passed her

last days under nurses' care far from home, her "stuff" now waiting to be claimed.

What's in a box is *your* treasure, *my* junk. What's in a box, a tri-
fle to you, the world to me. What's in a box, the essence of that
which another deemed worthy of preserving.

And yes, the box is metaphor; but while we laud those who
strive to think outside it, I decry those who forget what's inside,
lofty thinkers who don't know Jack. You don't need think-speak
from pretenders who never even bother to peek under that lid, to
look, to learn, to ponder what and why.

You see, what truly lives inside the box is some very good
thinking. It's the best of what legions before us conceived, then
tested and refined. It's the rules you learn so you can break them
judiciously for greater effect. It's the place with space when you're
ready to bring that imagination home.

It's where we keep Jack until the time is right.

I like to see thinking outside the box, but I trust it most from
those who prove they've mastered the art of thinking inside the
box, too. So keep an eye on what you know works, even as you
seek what might work ever better. Hold in, but look out!

I guess the best way to do that is: *Be the box.*

Achieve that, and the next big idea might just blow your lid
off.

FULLY RESTORED

An Essay by
Stephen Geez
StephenGeez.com
Photo by Scott Watson

I used to take an old Ford out for a spin.

Not a car, actually, she was an old lady.

Mrs. Ford would admit only to having passed her 90th birth-day, but she preferred a bit of mystery about her exact age. "A lady never tells," she teased, batting her eyelashes and offering a sweetly demur smile. Still, it's safe to say she had reached that point where one might call her a "vintage Ford."

I had just barely passed twenty myself, a university student. My Psychology of Aging class required a field practicum for anecdotal study of how our venerated elderly face the challenges of navigating a world increasingly geared to the young. This included me pairing with a local representative of the geriatric set, a chance to postulate sage truisms from spending a few hours with her twice a week.

Mrs. Ford had requested a nice young man with his own car, "getting out" being one of her priorities, which narrowed the student choices to me—my car, I mean, since the form offered no box to check indicating I'm "nice."

Mrs. Ford had outlived her only child, a son who'd given her a granddaughter, by then a young lady who had found her own place in a distant corner of the world. My case-study subject had opted to remain a part of her beloved Ann Arbor, a vibrant community both familiar and unrecognizable. Giving up her house, she'd found home in an assisted living facility, a regal old mansion in a stately west-side neighborhood, a room across the hall from her lifelong best friend who too soon after succumbed to failing health.

Mrs. Ford always wanted to go shopping first, her private stash of potassium-rich bananas requiring regular replenishment, and she liked to drive around to see how the city and campus were changing. She regaled me with myriad stories that breathed new life into places I'd looked at but never really seen. Then springtime tickled nature to life in the Huron Valley, and stopping to see the river proved one of her favorite sojourns, a way to restore some of the shimmer of youth to a vintage lady.

She once spoke of her late husband's shiny black Ford Model T, a car he stubbornly kept in the garage years after it had fallen into disrepair. I recalled just such a car parked forlornly in an overgrown barn on property adjacent to my grandparents' house in Tennessee. I found something reassuring in confirming with each childhood visit that I could look across the fence and see that old Ford parked there, telltale signs proving that despite occasional polishing it hadn't moved, somebody nevertheless unwilling to let it go. I suppposed that at least one story rattled around inside there, just as I suspected I would never hear it.

My summer after that semester with Mrs. Ford included a canoe trek across the South, the high point being a run of the rain-deluged White Oak Creek near where my grandparents had lived. I couldn't help but drive by for a gander at the old Ford.

I found empty barn—no car, the place cleaned up.

By then, that old Ford was probably worth more than its original cost, so I like to think somebody restored it to its former glory, then proudly took it somewere better for an occasional spin.

I spent the day floating with a friend, enjoying the glorious Tennessee hills until we happened upon a disturbing scene: remnants of an old car junkyard, rusting hulks pushed unceremoniously into the bank brush to rust and ruin, a secret revealed by the venerable old creek's unseasonal flood. The front end of a vintage Ford Model T lay mired in the muck, too far gone, its stories lost.

And I thought of Mrs. Ford.

She refused to let herself be shunted aside, left to rust and ruin. She signed herself up for the student program and sought opportunities not just to share her old tales but to make new ones about afternoons together chasing potassium-rich bananas and gazing appreciaitvely at a venerable old river that refuses to let secrets remain buried forever.

I would like to say that my initial interest in Mrs. Ford stemmed from a nobler purpose than earning credit, but I can't.

Nor can I say I succeeded in growing a long-term friendship with her.

No, when I returned in the fall, I learned that Mrs. Ford's time had too-soon passed.

Millions of old folks bide lonesome lives, even many who appear to be surrounded by crowds. You'll find them parked in fancy facilities, modern-day versions of the overgrown barn. The lucky ones delight in a bit of polish every now and then, lovingly tended by those who know the stories, or by those who look forward to making new ones.

Vintage people are not hard to find.

Just look, and with a bit of effort you, too, could take one out for a day.

Just like I used to take an old Ford out for a spin.

LYING IN WAIT

An Essay by
Stephen Geez
StephenGeez.com
Art by Dizzy

Some critters spend nearly their entire lives burrowed under dry stream beds and parched ponds, waiting for a rainy day. More than a few *people* have been known to exhibit similar behavior, also finding a spot to dig in and wait it out.

Most of the critters are amphibians, but you can find others, including but not limited to several kinds of reptiles. One of my favorites is a frog endemic to Africa. For most of the year, the climate and surrounding terrain are way too dry for it to survive, so it digs deep and lies in wait for better days, its metabolism slowed to borderline survival mode. This is one frog that lives on confidence, the conviction that if it can just hang on long enough, it'll catch a break.

And a break it does catch, except for those occasional cycles where exceptional drought does kill off all but the few hardiest specimens. Normally, the rains come once a year, a relentless deluge that turns into a gulley-washer and continues to rise to the category of full flood.

The water rouses our amphibians from their stupor, sparking a frenzy of "time to get busy." It's croakers galore, with everybody invited to the hip-hop dance. Whatever they've used their down time to plot and plan, now's their chance to make it happen, though in truth their agendas generally consist of mating to get that next generation laid and hatched, then eating as much as possible to store a year's reserve of fat. There's a bit of ribbety singing, frogly socializing, pushing and shoving over territory and partners, maybe some reminiscing about last year's sock-hop and how back in the day it seems the water tasted sweeter and pollywogs respected their elders . . .

Then, in what surely seems like no time at all, the water recedes, the flow turns to stagnant pools, the dance floor grows way more crowded, sparkle turns to muck as liquid dries, mud starts hardening, and the exhausted frogs—young and old alike—find places to dig in for another long year awaiting better days.

Their community is a lot like a town dependent on seasonal tourism. Most of the year, the residents of many vacation and spring-break destinations lie low, barely surviving, waiting it out. Then the key date comes, the weather breaks, the season opens, and a flood of visitors with cash-stuffed wallets and itchy credit cards washes in, good times for all. Locals put aside their worries and embrace the concept of *now or never* as they rake in enough to sustain themselves for another year.

Many businesses depend on a specific period to make most of their annual sales. That costume store losing money every month makes so much in October that it's worth burrowing in for long stretches.

Gift shops and other retailers mark their calendars for Thanksgiving to Christmas, hoping for a gulley-washer to float their enterprises through next summer's dry spell.

Farmers and growers of many stripes risk it all on a good crop, all the right conditions leading to a successful harvest.

I've known many people who also live their own lives like the desert frogs, but I can't say it's always a wise strategy. They burrow into someplace comfortable like a couch, then proceed to wait for the waters to bring in their ship. This usually amounts to avoiding the effort, the risk, the investment, the commitment to take advantage of whatever the world brings them, or to strike out and seek what they want and need.

I know childless couples now feeling too old to start a family, which isn't what they intended, but they just kept putting it off until after a promotion, more money, better place to live, options never good enough to achieve *just right*. Those frogs just figure it's time to hop to it and have a little faith; surely there's a way for the young'ns to muddle through.

I know people who woulda coulda shoulda started a business. They had the great idea, and could have pulled together the resources. Sure, they would have needed to fit some extra work time between busy minutes, but they sat idly by watching others do it with less.

I've known people who wanted to enhance their education, yet kept delaying for a better time, better funding, better opportunity, *better goals.*

I've seen people get engaged, then dawdle for years, refusing to set a date—or set a date years down the line. Is a *June* wedding really that important when nobody knows how much time each of you has? Do you really need another promotion or better job before you're *ready* to hitch? Isn't that rather like agreeing that *someday* you expect to be sufficiently in love to commit for life, but in the meantime it doesn't yet rise to that level?

Should you close your Halloween costume store in April?— or is it wiser to adapt to the calendar and bring in Easter decorations and supplies?

Should you wait for the water to rise, or turn on a hose and wash that gulley yourself?

We do have way more control over our circumstances than some lowly critters trying to survive in the same desert where they hatched and pollywogged their way to full frogdom, but even the best of us are subject to the whims of time and season and circumstance and fate. Do we find a seat on life's couch, wait it out, and miss even the greatest opportunities that float by? Or do we get up, get out, and make it happen to the best of our ability, working together when we can, working alone with no encouragement or support when we must?

In case you haven't noticed, life . . . is . . . short. The flood of opportunity comes only so many times before our time has passed.

Frogs know it: When the time comes, you *jump.*

Everybody's invited to the hippety hop.

Don't just sit on the couch till you croak.

ATTABOY!

An Essay by
Stephen Geez
StephenGeez.com
Art by Turtle

Attaboy!
    Interesting concept, that.
    My first recollection of the expression harkens back to hearing

my Uncle Norman talk about his new job. My father and I had joined him on his friend's houseboat for some lantern-lit, late-night crappie fishing during the willowfly hatch on Weiss Lake, a scenic patch of water nestled in the hills near Centre, Alabama. Norman had taken on new responsibilities at the Revere Aluminum plant near Scottsboro. Asked about increased compensation, he said, "Every time they give me more to do, all I seem to get for it is an *Attaboy!*"

When everybody laughed, he added: "Attaboy!s are fine, but you can't carry 'em down to the Piggly Wiggly to pay for groceries."

He certainly had a point. I mean, what is an Attaboy!? I guess you could say it's an acknowledgment of effort, a recognition of accomplishment, maybe even a thank-you for caring; but when it's time to pay for those groceries, you need something a bit more tangible than someone's approval or gratitude.

Yeah, just try handing out a few Attaboy!s and see what they get you.

Between baiting the hook and reeling in crappies, I thought about Attaboy!s I'd received. One stood out: My third-grade class had been assigned to write brief holiday stories. A bit longer and more elaborate than most, mine wove a tale in rhyming verse. Apparently this impressed my teacher, who circulated it among other teachers and administrators. Feeling it deserved a professional-looking presentation, the principal had his secretary type two copies, one for posting in the glass display case, one for me to keep. (Note: This reminiscence recalls the era of manual typewriters, a time when even adults rarely ever got to see their words "in print.")

Now, that was an Attaboy!—in tangible form. When the principal presented it to me in front of the whole class, everybody clapped, followed by many gathering around to *Oooh* and *Ahhh*, several wanting my autograph. I learned then that an Attaboy! you can hold in your hands not only makes it more real for you, but for others, as well. Yes, group Attaboy!s can be infused with a magical power all their own.

There is no limit to how one can bestow an Attaboy! Kids are usually happy with a simple thumbs-up, a gold star, a display of their creative efforts on the fridge . . . but you should never assume that's enough. Children can sense when Attaboy!s are doled out indiscriminately, but the mere fact of you issuing one is still better than indifference. Just bothering to look for opportunities proves you're paying attention, that you noticed, that you understand, that no matter how insignificant a simple act might be in the greater scheme, you were moved by it, and you want to acknowledge it.

I've received my share of Attaboy!s over the years, having been lucky to surround myself with people willing to make that effort. Many of the more symbolic forms of recognition, the awards and certificates and plaques, have been fun to display at various phases of life and career. Still, the first time a cadre of grinning executives slid an envelope across the table, a surprise merit-bonus check worth lots of groceries . . . well, let's just say the scuba-diving adventure it financed felt as tangible as the cool, fish-swirled water and hot, babe-splayed beaches of a most-excellent Attaboy!

I could offer a litany of more favorites, but as I ponder them, I keep coming back to one particular rather-poignant kind: surprise thanks, least expected, for a thankless job. When you volunteer your time and effort and resources to help others accomplish something for themselves, usually you have to *give yourself* the Attaboy! Even so, every now and then someone finds out what you've done, then makes it a point to remind you why it's all worthwhile.

Nothing beats an Attaboy! from the heart of someone who cares, a moment that passes right through you and leaves an indelible mark in ways you might not readily see, or which you might bring into focus only by looking closely through the prism of time and experience. I have to wonder if I would even be sharing this essay with you had I not as a third-grader held the school principal's Attaboy! in my hands and thought, Hey, putting ideas into thought-fully chosen words on paper can be quite cool, indeed.

Uncle Norman was grinning when he told his Attaboy! story. Even at that age, I could sense he felt good about his accomplishments, proud of his work. Though not exactly compensated with hard cash, I think he did, after all, get paid something more valuable—even longer lasting.

When you truly understand why it doesn't matter that most Attaboy!s won't buy groceries at the Piggly Wiggly, you might also notice that most don't cost anything to *give*, either. You could consider them investments in others' futures, but sometimes you might well see benefits unfold right then before your very eyes.

So consider all the people who pass through your life: loved ones who care what you think, strangers who work hard in service to you or others, and maybe, just maybe, a surprising number of good folks who try to make *your* world a better place. Might you be overdue to show them that you noticed? That you understand? That no matter how insignificant a simple act might be in the greater scheme, you were moved by it, and now you want to acknowledge it?

Don't count on buying groceries with an Attaboy!, but do try handing out a few anyway, and see what they get you . . .

You might just be amazed by what you get back.

UPHILL OR DOWN

An Essay by
Stephen Geez
StephenGeez.com
Image by Geez

I have lived atop the hill.
  And I have lived below.

258 Been There, Noted That / Stephen Geez

Some think this only matters when hiking in warm breezes or sledding on icy cold snows, but I think it's a difference that matters to everyone, a choice made by intent or default, whether or not one ever leaves the house.

I first noticed this distinction way (way way) back in college, my under-graduate years in Ann Arbor, living just steps from the entrance to Nichols Arboretum, the University of Michigan's natural preserve for native flora. "The Arb" sprawls across a stretch of the Huron Valley, encompassing the river and some bottomlands, a series of rolling hills ideal for peaceful strolls . . .

Or some raucous sledding when the world turns white.

I've sledded and tobogganed and skiied in more spectacular realms, hiked up and down mountains, and climbed cliffs until I found myself perched against the sky wondering whatever possessed me and *Now how am I going to get down?*, but there is something basic, something visceral about traditional sledding—no lines, no t-bars, no lifts, just you and the hill and a choice made after every run:

Shall I climb again for another?

It can be taxing, those long and wearisome treks up an ever-steepening incline, a ratio of effort at least ten times longer than every second spent zipping back down on one's favorite form of butt-rocket. Some won't do it, no quick thrill worth the exertion, delayed gratification not worth delay. Others will climb and keep climbing until they're exhausted, somehow finding as much fun in the trip up as the rip down.

So when you live near The Arb, your residence sits *above* the valley. Where most sledders must travel to a hill and start with that first climb, ending their day with a final ride down, Arborites start from the top and end the day with one last trek back up to go home.

I liked living at the top, and I'm always surprised by how many prefer to live every aspect of their lives at the bottom.

A man drives home after a long day, his gas tank nearly empty, motor running on fumes, and he passes the station, intending to fill up in the morning. Another stops, preferring to climb that hill before resting, thus anticipating a new day that begins at the top.

I actually know a young lady who keeps her dirty dishes in the sink. When she cooks, she washes what she needs, then leaves them dirty again, a clear example of bottom-of-the-hill thinking.

Many people live in debt, spending their way zip-bang down the slippery slopes knowing they'll have to work hard later to climb that pile of bills, a summit often rising higher than the initial slide. Others work hard to climb that hill first, then live at the top, allowing themselves occasional delights knowing they'll need to climb some more before they can ride again.

I've heard of "saving for a rainy day," but how about "working for a snowy day?"

Life sometimes presents opportunities, those rare confluences of circum-stance and fate, friends and family coming together un-expectedly, and invitation out of the blue. These are the mornings when a sparkling blanket of virgin snow presents itself, that in-stant when knowing you've already made the climb means now you can seize the day.

Most go through life worrying, preparing for the worst, buying insurance and developing all kinds of contingency plans, and this is smart planning, too, but what about preparing for the best?

What about working hard and finding joy in the very ef-fort? Remembering that every step up presents, not only a better view, but a possibility of the most unexpected chance to step off the edge and fly?

Every day we make these choices, by intent or default.

It's all in how we live.

I like the view.

Do you live at the top?

GENERATING

An Essay By
Stephen Geez
StephenGeez.com
Image by TheMan268

My great-grandfather lived past his 102nd birthday.
    I got to see him, too.

The old feller's longevity is a fact, recorded somewhere, I'm sure, and ver-ifiable. Intellectually, I consider this good news. It means one-eighth of my gene pool offers me good odds of inheriting more than a few crotchety years of my own. Consider, too, that a significant portion of his life occurred in the 1800s. Thriving back then proved even more remarkable than it should for me, given my access to modern medical care.

His name was Emanuel, which I only know because I called my father today to verify that and his age at death. Though woefully short of ready facts about his genealogy, I do hold a vivid image of him in my mind, even more than forty years since that rare day when we occupied the same room.

What saddens me about this memory, though, is something I wish more people would think about. You see, I don't recall actually talking to the man. I remember him more for where he was, how he looked, and the fact that he had gone blind. Sure, I was a youngster at the time, but I was more than old enough to hold my own in conversation with any interested adult.

My family had undertaken an out-of-state trip to catch up with kinfolk in Tennessee. One day while Mom and my siblings visited her sisters, my father took me to see his aunt and uncle and cousins in what, for me, proved to be a very different kind of world. We drove way out into the country, followed a rutted two-track, and wound up at what I believe can literally be classified as a *shack* in some overgrown Tennessee holler.

A gurgling creek, smelly outhouse, spring-fed concrete cistern, rusty old TV antenna atop a swaying pole—turn it by hand to get the other channel—and corrugated tin roof covering unpainted crude slat walls dominate my mental image of the exterior. Inside I see uneven Linoleum floors, old worn furniture, a flickering black-and-white console television, and lots of religious paraphernalia, especially a framed picture of Jesus on the wall and a crucifix scene built of abalone and other sea shells displayed atop the TV.

The old man sat in a chair in the crowded living room.

I guess it's possible I did get introduced, but all I recall is my father telling me who he was, then my great aunt explaining that he stayed with them now but used to live over to so-and-so, a reference I couldn't associate. As the child in this scenario, I spent much of the visit being seen-but-not-heard. Eventually I went outside and discovered that the creek hosted great numbers of a critter totally new to me: mud puppies—also known as mud dogs or water dogs. Good-sized slimy salamanders, or newts of some sort, they were. Those I remember vividly, too.

Four generations and six-hundred miles apart, I improbably overlapped with one of my ancestors at the same place at the same time for only one serendipitous occasion. If anyone even made him aware that he had a great-grandson whom he had never met, now standing right there in the room with him, it couldn't have been treated as much of a big deal, as it made no impression on me. I'm still fairly confident no introductions occurred.

I wish I could have a do-over.

Even now I find it amazing that I looked upon a living relative born in Confederate territory at the time of the *Civil War*.

When an older person dies and leaves behind grandchildren or great-grandchildren who are only a few years old, it saddens me to think the youngsters will have no real memory to preserve and share. Granted, in the years since my only exposure to a great-grandparent, we now have cheap and abundant means for recording people and hearing stories about the events in their lives. Sure, you can watch videos of Great-grannie all day, but that falls short of a vital link, flashes of understanding, a lasting connection.

What I would ask Great-gramps now surely would differ from what might have been on my mind as a youngster, but even if the best I could come up with at the time might be to wonder how he became blind and what that might be like, it still would have given me a chance to hear *him* tell it, to sense how *he* feels about it, to see if there might be anything *he* wanted me to know about him and how he lived.

Kids' memories are capricious and mischievous. In the moment, a youngster can amaze with the depths of her knowledge and insight, with his empathy and understanding. A dozen years later, though, or many decades down the line, nearly all of those day-to-day memories will have faded, merged, consolidated, re-associated, or largely disappeared for good. For me, the order of impressions from that day starts with people living in a stereotypical hillbilly shack in the woods, then catching mud puppies in the creek, the incongruity of a seashell crucification, that rusty antenna way way way up in the sky, and my great-grandfather . . . whose interesting characteristic seemed to be blindness.

In your sphere, there are some very old people, and some very young people. If the world works as it should, someday sooner than later the old people will be gone, and the young people will remember surprisingly little about them.

You can do something about that.

I'm not talking about the simple stuff, such as making introductions, showing an interest, carrying on a conversation. Nor am I talking about the fun-activity stuff; a day at Disney World with Gramps will likely imprint Mickey Mouse more vividly in a youngster's mind than recollections of who sat beside him during the Haunted Mansion ride.

What I am talking about is meaningful interactions offering opportunities to make indelible impressions and form enduring memories. Having an oldster record personal tales of the olden days is a wonderful idea, but it is academic to the youngest loved ones unless they are invited to participate. Let them plan the session, formulate the questions, *ask and react.*

Arrange for the oldster to teach the youngster something that will have meaning down the line. If the old guy custom-built furniture, they could start a birdhouse project together, a chance for him to pass along some skills and, more importantly, attitudes such as pride from producing woodwork with one's own hands. Half a century later, that youngster, since grown into a grandparent himself, will remember his own grandfather when he sees hand-crafted antique furniture, and he'll have a story to tell, a memory to cherish, a moment in time kept alive because someone cared enough to reach down through the generations and touch a child's heart.

If Great-grandma has a unique way of lovingly preparing special foods handed down through the generations, a faded recipe scribbled on a stained card pales before the exquisitely poignant opportunity for a curious little girl to learn for herself, not just the *how*, but the *why* these family traditions matter, why they deserve to be preserved, why who we are depends largely on the gifts entrusted to us during our brief time in the shining light between generations.

You in-betweeners not only can facilitate these opportunities, but also play a vital role in reinforcing the memories they produce. After an afternoon with Great Aunt Tildie, ask the youngster what he or she remembers most about the experience. Encourage him to imagine how he might feel about being old someday and having a young relative visit. Ask her if she will remember Aunt Tildie, and maybe tell a new generation about what it was like to share moments with a loved one who used to live very differently than we do today.

As a youngster, I often found myself thinking, *Wow, I want to remember this.* Read enough of my essays and you'll see I did notice a lot and make it a point to associate experiences with aspects of life that I guessed might be relevant again someday. However, I was an odd sort of kid, and many don't make that kind of effort. Today, most are so attention-swamped by our multi-tasking super-media world that they don't have much down-time for replaying memories and exploring the realm of introspection.

If you see grandchildren squandering a visit with the old folks by racing outside or disappearing into handheld media players, you're not trying very hard. It's worth competing for their attention. It's worth involving them in activities. It's worth empowering them to help write the agenda, to take charge of shaping the day's events. If they want to stare at a mini-screen, get a camera or recorder and ask them to help put together a fun presentation on what it's like when the old folks and young folks take a moment to delight in intersecting their worlds.

Yes, you might get some resistance, but if *you* want to be the one who is recalled someday, if you want new generations to look back and remember fondly how much *you* loved them, if you want them to know something of the even older loved ones *you* will be losing too soon, then generate those connections.

Someday off in the distant future, a new crop of old geezers will be glad you did.

And they'll love you for it.

GAME CHANGER

An Essay by
Stephen Geez
StephenGeez.com
Image by Geez

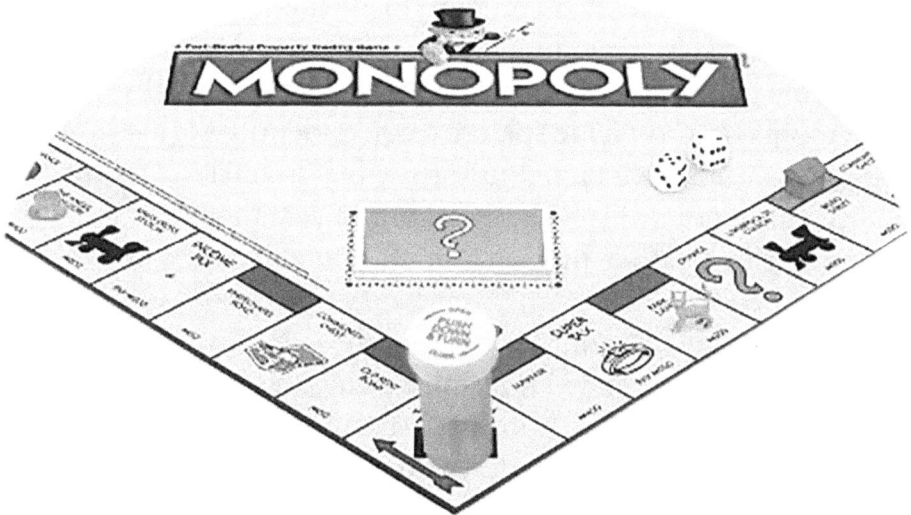

Sometime in my early teens, that age when it seems we'll live forever, I got to thinking about life expectancy, so I decided to play
a rather unusual game with myself.

I had read that as recently as a few hundred years ago even
those lucky enough to survive the high mortality rates of childhood rarely lived beyond their forties. I also kept noticing the

surprisingly young ages at which many historical figures had died. How much more could have been produced by those who were contributing to our collective understanding? We will never hear the treasures of Mozart composing as an old man.

Our life spans have lengthened considerably in the number of generations we count on our fingers, largely owing to advances in medical science. Sure, we can only imagine the upcoming breakthroughs that will stretch beyond our own brief time in the world, but we can and should rejoice in the sheer luck of being born in an era our ancestors would have considered miraculous for length and quality of life. I rely on modern medicine as much as anybody, but I don't take it for granted, and I hope you don't, either.

So the game I started playing during my junior-high years was this: monitor my own life span so I could identify the age at which my time would have ended if not for the "miracle" of a medical intervention not available a few hundred years ago.

Yes, it is a rather morbid notion, literally, and one with no obvious benefit. Call me the weird kid, if you want, but with me curiosity usually wins out, so I played the game for many decades to come. I even extended it to monitoring the life spans of those around me. It's not like I obsessed about it; I just filed the game in that mental in-box I clutter with inklings assigned peripheral awareness.

The game turned out not to be nearly as simple to play as I thought. The rules and definitions are not at all clear.

For example, when someone I knew would suffer an infected appendix that subsequently burst, I considered that *game over.* Not too many generations ago, neither the surgery nor the antibiotic regimen would have been available. This affliction routinely ended lives, and for most of history nobody even understood how or why.

In playing the game, though, I discovered that most of the calls are not nearly so easy to make. No one can possibly discern all the ways modern medicine has prolonged an individual life. For example, childhood vaccinations prevent illnesses that used to kill millions, even hundreds of millions. Whether or not you and I fall into the group saved this way, we can never know.

Even as we grow older, vaccinations continue to improve our odds. I missed my flu shot eight years ago, and that winter I fell so ill that I truly feared for my survival. I finally comprehended how influenza causes upwards of 300,000 hospitalizations and at least 10,000 deaths per year in the USA. I won't skip my shot again, yet I know several people who refuse theirs despite straddling several high-risk demographics, including old age and chronic health issues. I know one guy who refuses the vaccine for his small children even though both suffer juvenile diabetes.

Lucky for these people, when enough of the population is vaccinated, we achieve a high level of "herd immunity," meaning the most vulnerable are substantially safer because influenza does not infect enough viable hosts to spread nearly as much as it might. One friend brags that he doesn't *need* to get flu shots because he never catches the flu. I just tell him, "That's okay, I've got you covered. *You're welcome.*" Herd immunity complicates my game, though. I have no way of knowing how much *others* who embrace medical advances might have saved *me*.

Many of today's routine treatments are usually not considered life-saving, but we don't know for sure. In fourth grade my class watched a film depicting the first experimental treatments with penicillin, including a fourteen-year-old boy who suffered a compound fracture expected to prove lethal from the inevitable infection. Today we would not consider the injury life-threatening, partly because we have effective treatments and partly because vastly improved sanitation reduces our exposure to dangerous contagions. I don't count skin breaks vulnerable to infection as game-enders, but a few hundred years ago a mere cut might have risen to that level.

Other possible outcomes of accidental injury might be judged either way. Sometimes we are shocked that what appears to be a minor mishap becomes a fatality, maybe not right away, but as a direct result nonetheless. Maybe the simplest of modern medical interventions prevents death in many cases I would never have suspected as game-enders.

Even life-saving surgeries can be judgment calls. Someone dying from severe blood loss after a limb injury might well have been saved a few hundred years ago by crude amputation, even though the amputation-survival rate back then proved very low. A man who undergoes hernia repair not available in colonial times never can be sure if he saved himself from mere long-term discomfort or a subsequent bowel strangulation causing lethal gangrene, nor can he predict *when* the worst-case outcome would have struck and ended his game.

There are many ways modern medicine buys us additional life span we cannot measure. A woman who probably would have died of heart disease at around age fifty might prevent that with the installation of a stent at forty, but still die of complications at sixty. I can't say the stent saved her at forty, nor would I have any idea when in the next twenty years it started buying her extra time.

I also wound up considering the benefits of our modern civic infrastructure. Today we rely on calling 9-1-1 from anywhere anytime, then being whisked by a network of available ambulances on modern roadways to a nearby trauma center. Maybe then we are saved by minor treatment that was also available even hundreds of years ago, except that back then many helpless victims never would have reached professional treatment in time.

My game obviously became very complicated, so I decided to keep it as simple as possible: assume that every day I survive increasingly owes credit to modern medical science, whether I know it or not, and draw the line only when I can point to a specific, clear-cut woulda-died event.

I crossed that line in my mid-forties.

A passing kidney stone became lodged, which caused a rapidly spreading infection. I required two surgeries and a 30-day wallop of several powerful state-of-the-art antibiotics. The surgeon told me I came within 48 hours of sure fatality.

I finally identified my age, game over.

Some would say now I'm living on "borrowed time," but I haven't borrowed anything. I prefer to think of it as earned time, with full credit going to the human race's dogged determination to endure, and to our unique capacity for using science to transcend superstition, myth, and ignorance. We pursue clarity in our understanding of the real world, then devise an amazing array of means to bend it to our will, to make it work to our advantage. Survival is the quintessential drive, and we keep getting better and better at achieving it. In fact, we are so good now that another fundamental drive, procreation, is contributing to many problems from over-population.

Having crossed my own line, I now see that there is something to be gained from playing the game.

One unexpected benefit is that it encouraged me to notice— and try my best to avoid—the many ways people game the system *against* themselves. Sure, I've chased adventure to distant realms, from caves to coral reefs to mountain-tops to the sky, but I became a safety freak: thorough training, the best equipment, the sharpest team, back-up plans. I also avoided major health risks that in the politest sense might be called "counter-intuitive." Grateful that my uncle who suffered lung damage in a workplace explosion benefited from modern surgery, why would I willingly damage my own respiratory system choking on cigarettes for decades?

Still, the biggest benefits from playing the game surely must be *perspective* and *gratitude*. I am born into a time and a place where I *expect* to live well beyond my forties, the age I had read about as a young teen. I live among people who figure out how to make that possible, who build the infrastructure to make it accessible, who commit to ensuring that most of us receive the very best medical care available. Having grown acutely aware of how far we have come strengthens my faith that we will continue to move forward. I truly believe that despite the politics and the vested interests and the protectionism of so many have-mores, eventually *everyone* in my country will achieve the same access to the highest level of medical care, and that in time everyone on Earth will, too.

So, it turns out that my game is not over.

When *my* time came, it proved to be a game *changer*.

You see, now I'm living my second life. I don't think about it much, but I will take notice if the occasion arises for modern medicine to give me a third. Maybe I'll live a dozen lifetimes.

I will value them as more time to remember loved ones whose lives were cut short.

Maybe you will never experience that critical event where medical science clearly gives you a new life. Maybe you already have. I can't say whether you would feel better knowing you never needed the help, or if you would like finding poignant new appreciation in knowing you have sidestepped death.

Maybe you'll put the whole notion out of your mind, or maybe now *you* will start playing the game. Maybe you've already been playing it.

If you do decide to play, there is one rule that rises above all the others:

We win by taking care of each other.

Seriously. I'm a player, and I pledge my support for you, whether you consciously play or not. If I see you fall, I will pick you up, call for help, treat what I can, hold you until someone better prepared takes charge and tells me to step back.

I will continue to support medical research of every stripe

because it is one of the great aspirations of mankind. Many of us have favorite causes, something that has touched someone we love, but I believe in encouraging support for them all.

And as we continue learning how to prevent harm, how to ease suffering, how to cure what ails us, how to prolong life, we should work together to ensure that the help any one of us needs is available to us all.

That's a game everybody wins.

I'm a winner, and you're a winner, too.

I wish long and happy lives for you and everyone you love.

More Books by Stephen Geez

General Fiction
Dance of the Lights
What Sara Saw
Papala Skies
How It Turns Out

Media Thriller
Fantasy Patch

Mystical Adventure Series
The Fixer: *Crystal Clear* #1
The Fixer: *Spider Boxer* #2
The Fixer: *Hot Doggies* #3
The Fixer Graphic Flashback #1: *Shell Game*

Science Fiction
Invigilator
Zhasou Pure

Essay Collection
Been There, Noted That

GeezWriter
How-to Series for Writers

The Fresh Ink Group

Publishing
Free Memberships
Share & Read Free Stories, Essays, Articles
Free-Story Newsletter
Writing Contests

❧

Books
eBooks
FIG Bookstore

❧

Authors
Editors
Artists
Professionals
Publishing Services
Publisher Resources

❧

Members' Websites
Members' Blogs
Social Media

FreshInkGroup.com

Email: info@FreshInkGroup.com

Twitter: @FreshInkGroup

Google+: Fresh Ink Group

Facebook.com/FreshInkGroup

LinkedIn: Fresh Ink Group

About.me/FreshInkGroup

Fresh Ink Group

Frank relishes fast success and early retirement, but struggling to preserve his life's work thrusts him into a desperate battle to protect the people he cares about most.

Beverly seeks a new beginning in Tarpon Springs—until those she trusts steal control of her destiny, forcing a fight for her very survival.

All twelve-year-old Kevin wants is attention from the only man he respects, yet murder and the wrenching indifference of a callous legal system toward one vulnerable child proves even friendship might never be enough.

Riven by tragedy, consumed by grief, all three must confront the wondrous possibility that our indelible bonds may somehow transcend even death, that a cherished soul truly can find the way back.

Only together might this improbable family dare embrace their own brand of unexpected love, that infinite potential to achieve more than any one person can alone. Through it all, they are teased by the mystery of those dancing lights, a million pinpoints in every imaginable color swirling to form brilliant images of extraordinary lives.

FreshInkGroup.com

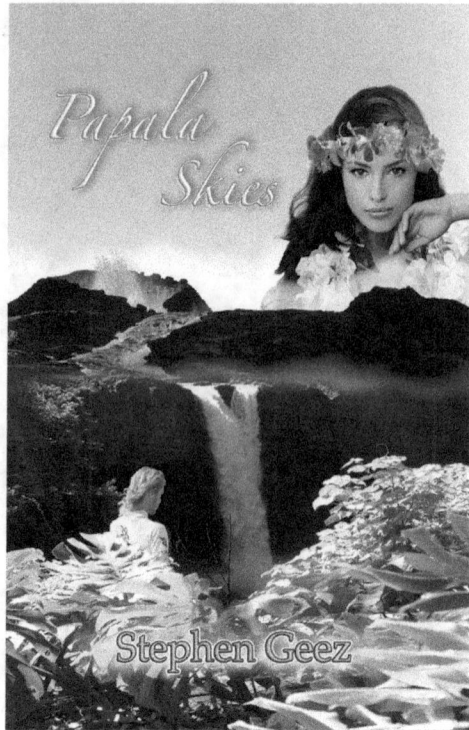

Chicago native Rochelle DuFortier likes to imagine the future, her world a series of picture postcards so vivid they sometimes seem real. When a foolish mistake at thirteen causes her mother's death, she's sent to a secluded Hawaiian valley, an outsider "haole-girl" among pidgin-speaking boys who hurl flaming papala spears under the full moon to summon her mother's spirit. After boarding school and a prestigious university back east, the ambitious young woman is torn between chasing new career opportunities, discovering her mother's heritage in a remote French village, and meeting obligations pulling her back to Hawaii.

On this island steeped in ancient mythology and modern superstition, Rochelle tests the possibility of sharing pieces of her life with those whose beliefs she barely understands and never intends to embrace. She dives the depths of a pristine coral lagoon, conceals bodies in a subterranean lava tube, and challenges the eruptions of a living volcano, even as she deciphers the truth about her mother's death and struggles to satisfy new debts born of old betrayals.

Will Rochelle lose what matters most, or might she learn what the smart octopus already knows?

FreshInkGroup.com

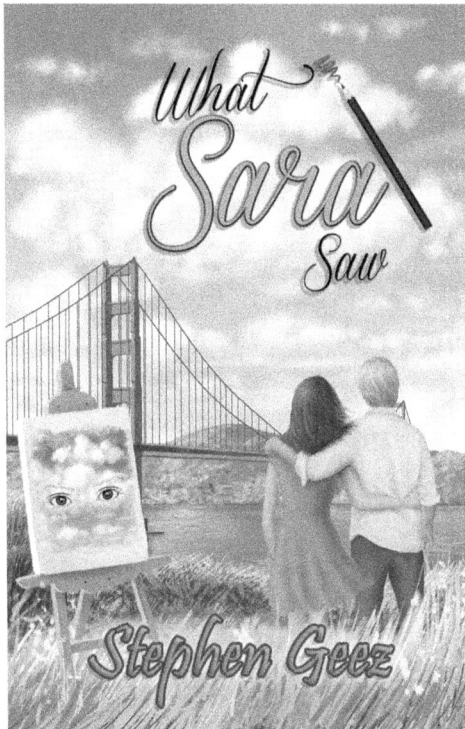

The boy looked back.

A simple pencil drawing, this depiction of a child watching from the reeds of a country pond frustrates and angers Geoffrey, unexpected reactions that stir Phrekka's lifelong passion for understanding the elusive power artists infuse in their creations.

Their only clue a "Sara" signature, the unemployed graphic designer persuades the enchanting Korean-American curator to help him discover more images by this enigmatic artist. From her world of privilege and mystical spiritualism to his of heartland farms and fundamentalist values, they will cross the country in search of the meaning in Sara's sketches, an odyssey to divine one extraordinary person's singular secret for touching people's souls.

Staggering revelations entangle them with issues of mortality and faith, sexuality and family violence, obligation and responsibility, deception and truth. Only by looking close at the dark and profane will they have any chance of coming together to create a legacy more beautiful than either ever imagined.

What Sara Saw paints exquisitely vivid portraits of two young people who must follow their hearts to recapture that innocent grace long lost to the whims of circumstance and fate.

FreshInkGroup.com